"It is nearly impossible to capture the stunning effect of *Just Research in Contentious Times*. In showing how critical PAR works, the chapters create a gut punch for research and its impact on participants and on the researchers themselves. It reveals that we are all guilty and also all vulnerable."

—**Yvonna Lincoln**, Texas A&M University

"*Just Research in Contentious Times* is beyond inspiring. The powerfully illuminating stories of suppressed progressive collective inquiry and radical theorizing revealed so imaginatively in this volume is vital for engaging youth and dispossessed communities in critical research methods for democratic movement building. This book is teeming with heartfelt practical examples of what knowledge production for human freedom and justice requires of us."

—**Joyce E. King**, Benjamin E. Mays Endowed Chair for Urban Teaching, Learning and Leadership, Georgia State University

"Michelle Fine's research captures both the results of structural violence as well as the miraculous forms of resistance undergirding the precarious daily life of society's most vulnerable citizens. Applying innovative methodologies, Dr. Fine synthesizes quantitative and qualitative data to privilege a ground-up rather than top-down analysis. This book offers the reader insight on how to capture a dynamic, balanced, and realistic portrait of people who face impossible odds."

—**William E. Cross**, professor emeritus, Graduate Center, CUNY

"This lucid, bold, and thoughtful book reconceptualizes what universities, education, and research can be. It is a record, too, of a staggering amount of difficult, often painful work. This—the sensitive, dogged, creative, and hopeful practices of collaboration, contest, and negotiation documented here—is what research as social justice looks like."

—**Corinne Squire**, co-director, Centre for Narrative Research, University of East London, UK

"In regards to methodology and epistemology, this is such a rich book. It can be read as a manifesto for a radical transformation of public education; as critical sociology of law from below; as a plea for a counter-hegemonic conception of human rights—the right to education in particular; as an experiment on critical participatory action research; as an exemplar of what I call the epistemologies of the south; and also as a brilliant and engaging intellectual autobiography."

—**Boaventura de Sousa Santos**,
University of Coimbra and University of Wisconsin-Madison,
author of *The Epistemologies of the South: Justice against Epistemicide*

"Fine exposes the veins, hopes, promises, and obstacles confronting scholars who dream of a racial democracy that is not yet here. For this we are in her debt."

—**Norman K. Denzin**, University of Illinois

"Michelle Fine's book is a provocative, scholarly, personal, and inspiring invitation to critical participatory research for justice. The examples of work with various marginalized communities, to gather evidence, challenge structural violence, and open up possibilities toward liberation, are perfect antidotes to dispassionate research that often bolster the status quo. Indeed, the entire book is a gripping, powerful, reflexive counter-story about research for justice and transformation—exactly what is needed in these contentious times."

—**Christopher C. Sonn**, Victoria University,
Melbourne, Australia

"Fine's writing is narrational, witty, charming, intellectually robust, and always deeply reflexive. A must-read that highlights the role of methodological creativity and pluralism in opening up vistas of imagined futures that are more just and egalitarian, and that are constantly unfolding. A quintessential, Fine piece of scholarship!"

—**Garth Stevens**, University of the Witwatersrand,
Johannesburg, South Africa

Just
Research
in Contentious Times

Widening
the Methodological
Imagination

MICHELLE FINE

TEACHERS COLLEGE PRESS

TEACHERS COLLEGE | COLUMBIA UNIVERSITY

NEW YORK AND LONDON

Published by Teachers College Press, 1234 Amsterdam Avenue, New York, NY 10027

Copyright © 2018 by Teachers College, Columbia University

Library of Congress Cataloging-in-Publication Data is available at loc.gov

ISBN 978-0-8077-5873-1 (paper)
ISBN 978-0-8077-5874-8 (hardcover)
ISBN 978-0-8077-7668-1 (ebook)

Printed on acid-free paper
Manufactured in the United States of America

25 24 23 22 21 20 19 18   8 7 6 5 4 3 2 1

The crisis consists precisely in the fact that the old is dying and the new cannot be born; in this interregnum a great variety of morbid symptoms appear.

—Antonio Gramsci,
Selections from Prison Notebooks

I think I want mostly to argue for a centrality of imagination because of its power to enable persons to reach towards alternatives, to reach beyond; and I want to argue for the arts because of the ways in which they open windows in experience, provide moments of freedom and presence, enable us to break with terrible moments of apathy and numbness, keep us, in our ongoing conversations with the young, ardently in the changing and problematic world.

—Maxine Greene,
Imagination and Becoming

Though we tremble before uncertain futures
may we meet illness, death and adversity with strength
may we dance in the face of our fears.

—Gloria Anzaldúa,
Borderlands/La Frontera: The New Mestiza

This book is dedicated to documenting the morbid symptoms and opening methodological windows to allow in the breeze of a more just tomorrow. As we engage humbly in research and in movements, on oppression and privilege, exposing structural violence and birthing radical possibilities, widening our imaginations for just research.

The essays in this book dance on the shoulders of so many no longer, who nourished the passions in the volume and made me laugh: Rose and Jack Fine, Thea Jackson, Linda Powell Pruitt, Jean Anyon, Maxine Greene, Ethel Tobach, and Morton Deutsch. Your collective ghostly presence lingers lusciously on every page.

Contents

Preface

Saturday morning in the fog of mid-January 2012, I read to my mom Rose, age 96, drifting away, excerpts from a book compiled by Tillie Olsen, *Mother to Daughter/Daughter to Mother* (1984). Kathy Boudin had sent me the book, a compilation of letters from mothers to daughters/ daughters to mothers, written by women writers and poets. I believe her mother gifted the book to Kathy, and years ago, over the phone from prison, Kathy read excerpts to her mother, accompanying her as she weakened and approached death.

And so I lay in my mother's arms in Teaneck, New Jersey, speaking aloud what I think I remember to be Zora Neale Hurston's entry in Olsen's book, about her mother at death's door, a gauzy memory of Hurston's words: "Her mouth was slightly open but her breathing took up so much of her strength that she could not talk. But she looked at me, or so I felt, to speak for her. She depended on me for a voice" (Olsen, 1984, p. 195).

And my mother spoke in a very weak voice,
"I have so many stories, Michelle."
Grabbing for a pen, "Mom, tell me."
"Oh, no, I can't."
"Why can't you?"
"They are written on my heart. You tell."

And so I write. . . .

A STORY OF CRITICAL INQUIRY: DEMOCRATIZING KNOWLEDGE

This story begins in Chapter 1, an autobiographic reflection that stitches together the crossroads of my growing up—a tangle of immigration, White working-class aspirations and struggles, maternal sadness, paternal mobility, and the story of the chubby youngest watching, in preparation to write this book 60 years later. This chapter is rooted in what might be called autoethnography, reflecting on a life as it refracts, embodies, and resists across a range of historic moments, within a distinct geographic space. Here is a white working-class girl, from a Jewish immigrant family, "becoming White" in the 1950s at the margins of suburban America, and then working within and against the institution we know as the academy and the practices we know as research. It is a daughter-of-immigrants' story—White immigrants—where I listened intently and painfully to my mother in bed, and watched with desire and envy as my father walked out the front door to America. This is the story of accumulated privilege, and a humble never-enough commitment to research as resistance and imagination.

Across Chapters 2 through 6, my research biography joins with others—most notably critical scholars at the Public Science Project—amplifying these early embers of insight/incite. Across three decades, María Elena Torre, director of Public Science Project, and I have been committed to listening to smothered voices, and to contesting privilege, challenging expertise, and asking whose knowledge is considered legitimate. We have committed to revealing the wounds of state, corporate, and intimate violence and also the resistance, humor, and soft sanctuary collectives where marginalized youth nest. We draw from feminist, Marxist, critical race, and post-colonial theorizing. Over 30 years I and we have listened intently to voices smothering under covers, exiled from schools, locked up in prison, growing up amidst Islamophobia and homophobia, deported or fearful of leaving the house. And I have tried to understand how others can ignore the screams. Theorizing and attaching these voices, always, to histories and structures, movements and struggles, never allowing the story to sit alone, I write, and with others we organize through policy, theory, art, community work, movement work. . . .

Chapter 2 draws from a series of ethnographic and mixed-methods projects conducted with school pushouts and with Muslim American youth, tracing the critical voices of "exiles within." My history in a family of welcomed exiles contrasts sharply with the spiky violence imposed on those exiled from within—from schools, the economy, and the nation-state—especially but not distinctly, today. This research collects stories spoken from "wild tongues" and "lives at the rim," nourished in the in-between, what Gloria Anzaldúa (1987) called "the borderlands," where cultures, identities, and conflicts clash, and sometimes birth new meanings. With friends and colleagues at the Public Science Project at the Graduate Center, City University of New York

(CUNY), we lean on Anzaldúa to think about how, in critical participatory projects, we co-produce knowledge with people who know too much about structural violence and exclusion, who carry histories of silenced knowledge, who understand the footprints of U.S. "progress"— from below.

All of the projects sketched in this volume were designed within a research assemblage, including at different points youth, women in prison, women and men no longer in prison, activists, advocates, working-class families, lawyers, policymakers, researchers, artists, and educators. The projects have been designed to speak back to the law, theory, social movements, and community life.

In Chapters 3 and 4 we consider two research projects crafted in deep collaboration with lawyers and with youth attending highly disinvested schools, for admission as expert testimony to the courts. The projects showcased in these chapters were undertaken in California class-action lawsuits brought on behalf of children of color and poverty who had been systematically denied equitable education and subjected to the structural violence of disinvestment, denial of human rights, and mandated miseducation. We gathered narratives from young people attending hugely under-resourced schools, placed these narratives in the structural and historic design of underinvested public education and the existent literatures, and aimed to convince judges that their decisions could alter policy, structures, institutions, and lives—in a profoundly unjust world.

I ask your generous indulgence as you read these essays; imagine how we tried to "curate" lives of state betrayal, in the belly of the State, in a courtroom, to animate both oppression and agency, seeking to convince a judge that radical transformation of public education is possible, in a system long plagued by, and in large part designed to reproduce, significant racial and class disparities, always seasoned with spaces of radical possibility.

In Chapter 3 (with April Burns, Yasser A. Payne, and María Elena Torre), you will read our expert report, submitted in *Williams v. California*, and you will see, hear, and feel how much low-income children of color desire education that challenges and nourishes, and how rarely they get it. In Chapter 4 (with A. Cory Greene and Sonia Sanchez), you will read another essay, also produced after collaborating with lawyers, where we spoke with and collected maps of "draw what TIME feels like in your body in school," from scores of children and educators. In this case, we decided we would not participate in a lawsuit calling for extra learning time for highly marginalized children attending highly dysfunctional schools that, as Jose mentioned, "mostly feel like prison." While neither project was "classically" participatory, our research design, analysis, and interpretations were deeply informed by the young people, educators, activists, and lawyers with whom we collaborated. And because the transcripts of all of our interviews were fully available to the attorneys arguing against more money or more time, and arguing that expanded resources for poor children in disinvested schools would be wasteful, we had to be extremely precise in our analytic and interpretive decisions. These cases provoke important questions about the possibilities and limits of critical policy research. (For a rich discussion of the promise and pitfalls of critical policy research in education and criminal justice, see Sandwick, Fine, Stoudt, Torre, Greene, & Patel, forthcoming).

Chapters 5 and 6 sketch the contours, delights, and troubles of critical participatory research in varied educational settings—schools, prisons, communities, and popular education workshops. Chapter 5 unearths a long and buried history of community-based participatory research projects initiated in prisons, in coalmining communities of Tennessee, in schools and youth organizations, re-membering the legacy of critical research in which we walk, and explores two critical participatory projects designed across sites, in the United States and transnationally. Both projects document the grotesquely uneven distribution of educational opportunities even after significant judicial and international decisions for educational justice became law: "Echoes of *Brown*" was developed by intergenerational research teams across a series of desegregated schools to trace the unfulfilled promise of *Brown vs. Board of Education* in the United States, and "Do You Believe in Geneva?" was designed across a transnational set of youth organizing projects to trace the disparate implementation of the United Nations Convention on the Rights of the Child, in terms of educational policy. Both studies sought to document, contest, and provoke alternatives to the vastly uneven landscape of educational opportunities. The evidence in both projects was to be presented to policymakers in local school districts and to the Geneva Human Rights Commission, respectively. When compared to our initial intent, the research stories unfold in wildly divergent paths, including a deliberate move toward performance of the evidence, and a retreat from the "fantasies" of interested school boards, or even Geneva.

Chapter 6 details "What's Your Issue?" a bold, intergenerational, and participatory project, with a mixed-methods design, including a national, participatory survey designed by, for, and about LGBTQ and

gender-nonconforming (GNC) youth and ten local ethnographic in-
vestigations across the United States. The WYI survey gathered quantitative and qualitative perspectives from more than 6,000 LGBTQ/
GNC (gender non-conforming) youth ages 14–24, over-sampling
youth of color and transgender nonbinary youth, about their dreams,
desires, betrayals, struggles, activisms, and agendas for justice across
all 50 states, Puerto Rico, and Guam. This project opens significant
theoretical, political, and ethical questions about young people's rejection and explosion of traditional identity "categories" and their lack of
desire to "assimilate" or "be tolerated." We hear a fierce insistence on
recognition and demands for transformation. You will feel their "willful subjectivities" and "radical wit," their commitments to multiple
selves and powerful solidarities.

The Conclusion positions Critical Participatory Action Research as
a humble tool in contemporary movements for justice and democracy.
This final essay places the "science question" squarely in times of rising
inequality gaps, accumulation by dispossession, spikes in hate crimes,
White nationalism, and voracious corporate greed. I argue for critical
public science undertaken with and by communities and movements
as a strategy for building critical consciousness, archiving local knowledges, and forging surprising solidarities. The Conclusion muses about
"to whom" we are and should be accountable as we undertake critical
inquiry in revolting times.

A WORD ABOUT
WORDS AND METAPHORS

In 1944, Aime Cesaire, Martiniquais poet and philosopher of the Negri-
tude movement, delivered a lecture in Haiti in which he offered a gift
to the audience: "Poetic knowledge is born in the great silence of scientific knowledge" (1990, p. xlii).

With gratitude to Cesaire, I offer a (p)reflection on language, words,
and metaphors. Throughout this volume I am in conversation with
many long gone, particularly radical scholars of color, who have educated and moved me with text, but/and also with intimate ghosts of
various hues who touched my life with science, philosophy, critical
theory, matzo ball soup, and laughter. I write and speak in a pidgin
of science and poetry; I don't always intend that, but people tell me
so. I conjure metaphors to provoke slightly more than the empirical
can reveal, often slightly sexual (thanks, Dad). The metaphors hold

the affect, the irreal, the sensuality of experience that can't/won't be contained, simply observed, or documented on the page.

The metaphors are rooted in biography and desire; they rise from my belly to my tongue to my fingers. Many have been borrowed from young people good enough to sit on benches with me over 30 years. I try to credit them for all they have taught me, as I pass their language on to you the readers, who should cite them, and not just me, as you cultivate your own ideas. These metaphors are mine/ours; boundaries have never been my strength. As readers—students, activists, researchers, organizers—feel free to shoplift, or better yet, find your own metaphors. They are loitering in your head, stuck to your heart, floating around your belly. Those of us who are White researchers walk in a long and shameful history of story-lifting, hawking stories of Black/Brown pain and pocketing the profits. We must be exquisitely careful about over-borrowing and under-crediting—stealing—the words, stories, or metaphors of others, especially people of color. Those of us who are White have an obligation to excavate critically our own her/his/their stories of privilege to understand how we sit in tragic dialectics with structures of oppression, and how we might replace ourselves within solidarity movements of resistance. Even those of us who are kind of nerdy, critical researchers.

Acknowledgments

I write with so much appreciation for those I love, who have been good enough to be in conversation and collaboration with me over the years, in so many ways: David, Sam, Caleb, and Demetrius, love you all, and always. Sherry and Richard, can't imagine life without you. María Elena Torre, I have no words, just grace, appreciation, and love. With gratitude and respect for years of friendship, tears, and laughter, wandering through theory, the land mines of participatory research, and the struggles of organizing for justice—in no particular order so you have to read them all—Nancy Barnes, Maddy Fox, Brett Stoudt, Monique Guishard, Yasser Payne, Lori Chajet, Jennifer Ayala, Anne Galletta, Bill Cross, Donnie Cook, Lois Weis, April Burns, Rafi Torruella, Debora Upegui, Eve Tuck, Alyssa Bowen, Janice Bloom, Rachel Liebert, Mayida Zaal, Sara McClelland, Sarah Zeller-Berkman, Susan Opotow, Susan Saegert, Leith Mulling, Katie Cumiskey, Jason Van Ora, Bernadette Anand, Carlton Jordan, Caro Munoz-Proto, Steph Anderson, Wen Liu, Akemi Nishida, Allison Cabana, David Frost, Emerson Brisbon, Caitlin Cahill, Tamara Buckley, Deb Tolman, Rod Watts, Puleng Segalo, Thea Abu El Haj, Linda Brodkey, Perry Gilmore, Sandy Silverman, Julie Blackman, Jill Bradbury, Ruth Hall, Linda Tuhiwai Smith, Jared Becker, Carmita Rutling Champ, Ginny Vanderslice, Garth Stevens, Corinne Squire, Edwin Mayorga, Lauren Wells, Sean Massey, Carla Marquez, Pedro Pedraza, Molly Andrews, Regina Tuma, Kathy Boudin, Jessica Ruglis, Wendy Luttrell, Ofelia Garcia, Patricia Clough, Suzanne Ouellette, Judith Clark, Cheryl Wilkins, Iris Bowen, Jude Kubran, Alexis Halkovic, Leigh Patel, Migdalia Martinez, Donna Hilton, Pam Smart, Rosemarie Roberts, Melissa Rivera, Ann Cook, Debbie Meier, Margo Okazawa-Ray, Amy Hass, Pearl Rosenberg, Sunil Bhatia, Louise Kidder, Catherine Lhamon, Mark Rosenbaum, Kathryn Eidmann, Cindi Katz, Lori Chajet, Janice Bloom, Lin Walker, Reva Jaffe-Walter, Donna Cangelosi, Melissa Rivera, Mike Fabricant, Selcuk Sirin, Stephanie Urdang, Valerie Futch Ehrlich, Talia Sandwick, Celina Su, Dayna Cunningham, Heidi Dorow,

Sanjiv Rao, Jeanne Oakes, Cory Greene, Dana Ain-Davis, Steven Fine, David Fine, Jackie Fine, Stan Karp, Gayl Shephard, Latifah Jannah, David Heron, Chris McGoey, Lynn Fedele, Michelle Billies, Joyce King. *Abrazos* . . .

To the generous souls who midwife words into books at Teachers College Press, I am forever in your debt: Carole Saltz, Peter Sclafani, and Susan Liddicoat.

CHAPTER 1

Loss and Desire

Bearing Witness in White, Working-Class, Suburban New Jersey

I begin my methods courses with a simple thought: We have an obligation to ask, from where do our questions originate? And then we know, to whom we are accountable.

Suburbia, circa 1955.

"You walk into the house and first thing you see is a toilet?"

The bathroom sat directly inside the doorway of 510 Summit Street, more evidence of our failure to exit the working class. My mother would prefer you not look at the bathroom. No, turn right please. Glide down
    four
            steps
                into
                    the
                        sunken living room;

                        a grand entrance, signaling mobility.

My memory pulls back to the door. I don't remember if it was heavy or not; metal or wood. Probably metal with a cursive F tucked into a circle, smack in the middle of the door. The door was my childhood transitional object; connecting and separating me from the world; progress from the Depression; us from the *Goyim*. (Yiddish: non-Jews.)

Each morning, before I was old enough to attend school, my three-, four-, and five-year-old eyes followed as Daddy, Sherry, and Richard left for America. From my TV perch, with a bowl of sugary cereal in my lap, I watched, as I cared for and was cared for by my mother, in bed often, riddled with headaches. Later in the day she would emerge, and together we would watch as Penny negotiated life on *As the World Turns*. The wet *shmatta* (Yiddish: rag) on her head carried the secrets of generations of women—their desires and losses.

1

My mother called our home *"the cemetery."* I often wondered how many of us were buried there.

At least until 6:00 p.m.

Then, most nights, when we heard his key in the door, we ran to greet my father. Sweaty with an acrid aroma of pipes, trucks, copper nipples and elbows, his body carried traces of a plumbing supply shop, seeping through his flannel shirt. As these seductive new smells of America—money, working-class masculinity, and possibility—swept in, we lined up like ducks waiting for our pecks. Standing tall and smiling, we were the evidence, his receipt for the voyage to America.

If my father didn't exist, capitalism would have had to invent him. Poor immigrant Jew sells junk in a horse and buggy on the Lower East Side, goes to war, and makes good.

A few nights a month/year, Dad would drive home in his truck. The words *Rockland Plumbing Supply* were spray-painted on the side. And every time he drove it home, the police would arrive. That is, Mrs. Sternberg would call the police. Dad would answer the door, and Mom would hide behind him and ask (in a stand-by-your-man kinda way), "What's wrong with the plumbing truck?" She'd always pronounce the B, *plumBing,* much to our collective shame. "No commercial vehicles in the neighborhood." My father knew that, and drove it home anyway.

We hated the Sternbergs. They hated us. And they were one of the few Jewish families in the area. They were rich. We were *"traif"* (Yiddish: unkosher; impure; disgusting), ghetto, greenhorn.

We didn't mow the lawn very often. In fact Richard, my older brother, wanted to pave it and put in a basketball court.

Cousin Bobby would arrive at our house well after midnight, driving in from his army base in Texas, in a car on its last legs. He'd sleep in there 'til morning.

Sundays we had the *"gantseh meshpokah"* (Yiddish: entire clan) for barbecues. Lots of large-breasted women and short men. The women were loud, and the men were all sleeping in one room, on their one day off from chasing the American dream.

We were just the wrong kind of Jews. The margin of the margin—a useful space for daydreaming and theory building.

FAMILY HIS/HER-STORIES

In 1921, my parents sailed as children on separate disease-infected and dream-infused boats, from Poland to the "green lady" in New York harbor, with and without parts of their families who knew too well the price of living through a pogrom. They were sliding into America just under the rapidly falling immigration wire, drifting into the landscape at a moment in history when the "Jews "became White folks," as described by Karen Brodkin (1998).

Seven-year-old Rose Hoffer, my mother, was the baby of an orthodox Jewish family of 18, or 16, or 15 births—depending on who was counting, and whom was counted. She came to Ellis Island accompanied by two brothers (Moishe and Hanshel), a sister (Rachel), and Rivka, her 55-year-old mother (*"Who knows how old she was? No one from Europe knows how old they are!"*). The moves of war ruthlessly yanked and distorted the borders of nations and emotions, carving out ghettos of trauma and blood.

At age seven, Jack Yankelovich also traveled to the United States, Harlem in fact, with his grandmother. This was four years after he was "given up" by his young widowed mother whose second husband "didn't want a child who wasn't his own." ("How did you feel about that, Dad?" asks the aspiring psychologist baby daughter of Rose and Jack, circa 1975, just entering graduate school. "Never thought about it, baby.")

This amazing, proud man had a laser-like focus on the future. And no rearview mirror. Years later my father would learn that his mother, stepfather, and stepbrothers were eventually killed, left behind in the Polish ghettos to be crushed under Nazi boots. My father never spoke pain or sadness; those were exiled emotions left on the other side of the ocean. Directed and passionate, he was thoroughly dedicated to a better life for us. Narrating a life of blissful mobility, his capillaries quietly filled with the cholesterol of denial, eventually—at age 85—choking his heart. Note to reader: My father was a good guy; he really wanted a feminist daughter, but not a feminist wife.

My mother graduated from Eastern District High School in Williamsburg, Brooklyn, married her sweetheart, and together they danced the anniversary waltz from poverty on the Lower East Side to plumbing-supply suburbia. For years she undressed in the middle of the day, to put on a *schmata* when she came home from shopping. For 61 years she loved being Mrs. Jack Fine, never learning to write a check, use a credit card, or order for herself in a restaurant. She drove only once—with me—that was enough.

In the 1960s and into the '70s, Dad continued to declare himself captain of the ship. When I was 16, in 1969, I responded to this angrily; feminism was sailing. I defended Mom's rights as a woman, while she was busy mopping the ship's deck and caring for her captain's hats. From college I would write letters home to *Ms.* Rose Hoffer (only after my first women's studies course), and the letters would be returned, unopened, stamped Addressee Unknown. I was/am hinged to Rosie; we share stretch marks. This relation is, of course, inscribed in my research practice, my intimate relations, my political engagements, and my most neurotic self.

My mother's life and body carried the joys and the burdens so typical of upwardly mobile White working-class women of the '50s and '60s, weighed down in depression, loving her Jackie, caring for children, a nervous wreck, filled with secrets, shame, desire. She and I obsessively watched *As the World Turns* and *Queen for a Day*, the only sources of evidence of lives truly lived, yearning for a life outside the constraints of White shame, hetero-constraint (these are my words, of course, sorry, not really hers), the sweet side of patriarchy . . . but back then we just called it "migraines."

But inside that body burned a soul of humor, passion, humanity, the sum of which I was stunned to hear, in an uncharacteristically sophisticated, fully Americanized dialect of desire, spoken faintly from her deathbed, this past January, when she was a sweet puddle of Yiddish, breasts, laughter, and slumber.

Living within 10 miles of the Palisades Amusement Park and within 10 years of the end of the Holocaust, we too rode the roller coaster of assimilation, strapped in with ambivalence, shame, and pride. Our original family name, *Yankelovich*, was butchered at Ellis Island, and came out *Fine*. My sister taped down her nose at night so it wouldn't grow. My brother Richard got TB in high school. The only kid who did. They told me it was a broken leg. Just one of a million family secrets. *"Who needs to know?"* my mother explained decades later when I inquired about his lengthy hospitalization.

Dad refused to join a synagogue even though Mom yearned for a community, longing for the melodies of her Orthodox childhood. And of course he remained fluent in all the prayers up until his death. The living room sofa was covered in plastic. No mess you can't wipe away. My mother baked *tzimes* (carrot pudding) with marshmallows dripping off the sides. And we proudly celebrated Christmas: tree, tinsel, and balls.

Mom never ate dinner with us, that is, she never sat. *"Who can sit?"* (Much to my embarrassment, I didn't notice this until well into my 20s, when David, my partner, said, "I'm not eating this food until she sits and eats it first.") Dinner was served in the dining room.

I mean to say, Mom served us dinner in the dining room, once Dad came home. *Never trust the passive voice; it hides her labor and his privilege.* The warm glow of sunset blanketed us, surrounded by floral wallpaper. I loved that wallpaper, stained with the grease of marrow-bones and chicken necks and feet, and Minute Steaks, circling my tongue and my memory. The grease slid up into the middle class with us. To this day I still love marrowbones. I've been known to sneak into a Thanksgiving kitchen to rip off and devour the juicy, killer turkey butt.

The fat of childhood keeps me connected to and repulsed by that home. The not-so-silent B, the unruly lawn, cousin Bobby, the wet rag, her migraines and depressions, our days marinating in the working class, skipping into the solid middle class, White-skin privilege, the truck, the loss and pain of what was left behind, all surface in my work.

TRACING THE BIOGRAPHY OF OUR RESEARCH QUESTIONS

I have been bequeathed, then, to ask two questions, over and over in my research, my teaching, and my activism; in schools, communities, prisons, and youth social movements:

- Where in the body, the family, the culture, the nation and in the globe do bodies of sadness swell and fester in the shadow of progress?
- And, then, where lies the missing discourse of desire? (see Fine, 1988)

In most households we find a social psychological diaspora of emotional bodies. Some carry and speak the unbearable weight of loss; others bury, deny, and silence. The youngest, chubby child, lucky to be born when the family financial profile was approaching a middle-class smile, always a watcher and a performer, I tracked my mother's migraines that moved deeper and deeper into her body as our family "made it." Only she could embody what the rest of us were forbidden to speak.

Where does loss hide away when progress walks in the door?

This question would carry me to circuits later in my writing life.

My stance as critical participatory researcher has matured in the soil of a thoroughly immigrant Jewish family, a working-class home filled with love but not books, and then deep involvement in feminist, antiwar, and antiracism struggles, eventual privilege. I am the mother of a very diverse group of boys/young men—Demetrius, Sam, and Caleb (two by C-section and one by foster care); the partner in a 30-year love affair with David (we never married, refusing yet another institution that legitimates "some"—couples and children—while casting a long shadow of "illegitimacy" on others); teacher and learner with scores of graduate students and colleagues from the University of Pennsylvania and the Graduate Center at the City University of New York. And I'm funny.

COMMITMENTS OF CRITICAL RESEARCH

My dual genetic lines endowed me with the "*chutzpa*" (Yiddish: *nerve*) to theorize and study the visible and cellophane lines of power and (in)justice that stretch from the political to the psychic, by way of the social psychological. Situated in prisons, schools, and communities, using participatory methods and commitments to decolonizing knowledge, drawing on feminist, Marxist, queer, and critical race theory, the work tracks empirically the capillaries of racial, sexual, classed, and gendered injustice. I document the rage, despair, and migraines, tracing too the ripples of resistance and flames of desire. While my work maps a geography of shame and desire, each project holds my little autobiographic secret—that those persons and affects most viciously exiled are the soul of our moral community and they embody not only pain but desire; that privilege is relentless, and fragile, and maybe that's why it is so defensive—ever aware of, and ashamed by—its dependence on Others.

The community-based research projects have been designed to trouble the common sense about unjust arrangements that seem so natural or deserved; to destabilize what we think of as "normal"; and to reveal where resistance gathers and where radical possibilities might flourish (see Ayala, 2006; Fine et al., 2003; Fine & Torre, 2004; Fine, Weis, Pruitt, & Burns, 2004; Fine, Weis, Wong, & Weseen, 2000; Fox & Fine, 2012; Payne & Brown, 2016; Stoudt, Fine, & Fox, 2011/2012; Stoudt et al., 2015; Zaal, Salah, & Fine, 2007).

Using qualitative and quantitative methods, always in deep and fraught participatory collectives, my colleagues and I aim to document, across our varied projects, what Nell Painter (1995) has termed "soul murder." We cultivate evidence of activism and challenge, as well as what James Scott (1990) has called the "hidden transcripts of resistance." We return a critical analytic gaze to the social arrangements, institutions, distributions, ideologies, and social relations that reproduce and legitimate everyday injustice. Our "research camps" include activist elders, youth, women in prison, students in over- and under-resourced schools, Muslim American adolescents. Together we write and perform scholarly and popular re-presentations of individuals and groups that have long been demonized in the culture, held responsible for their own struggles, and blamed for larger social problems. Some scenes follow.

In Prison

June, 2001: A collective of feminist participatory action researchers gathered to reflect on our work at Boston College. María Elena Torre and I spoke that night for/with/despite those who were "otherwise detained"—our friends and co-researchers, Kathy, Iris, Judith, Donna, Migdalia, Missy, Pam, still behind bars. Specifically we spoke about "Changing Minds," a participatory research project at Bedford Hills Correctional Facility, a maximum security prison for women, where our research team of seven women in prison and five of us not, came together to study the impact of college in prison, or the meanings of freedom inside hell, or the collusion of racism and sexism in the lives of women of color in prison, or how their babies sleep at night in the Bronx without their moms (see Fine et al., 2003).

Maria and I described participatory action research (PAR) behind bars, under surveillance, in the warm, fictional comfort of a space of women, in a college in a prison in a nation with 2,000,000 behind bars. At 10:57 a.m. on Tuesdays, some of our research team rushed to leave; some had to stay. We all flinched. Critical research among women, in a tense little corner behind bars, in prison, "interrogating" and "theorizing" college, T-tests, analyses of variance, Spanish, sex, stories, voices, danger and pleasure, guilt and redemption. Only some of us are allowed to hold the tape recorder. Others had their cells searched last night . . . poetry journals confiscated. We dare not speak of our hatreds or outrage; we may go nuts, slowly, individually, or as a collective.

Deep into our work, probably 3 years in, we were writing up our final report and talking about how to write about our participatory research team. Neither wanting to flatten power issues nor reify the differences between insiders and outsiders, we struggled to craft the section on who is the "we" of the research collective. I naively offered:

"What if we write something like, 'We are all women concerned with violence against women; some of us have experienced, most of us have witnessed, and all are outraged.'"

To which Donna said, "Michelle, please don't romanticize us. Your writing is eloquent, but you seem to have left out the part that some of us are here for murder."

Another woman extended the point, "And some of us for murder of our children."

The argument was growing clear. "When we're not here, in the college, and we're alone in our cells we have to think about the people affected by our crimes. We take responsibility, and we need to represent that as well as our common concerns as women, as feminists, as political . . ."

Maybe like my father I was trying to tell a sweet story of "we"—hiding the blood and the pain.

In Israel/Palestine

Academic year 2006–2007: I was on sabbatical and invited, by a group of Arabs in Israel, to spend time at the Institute for Jewish and Arab Studies at Haifa University. I had never been to Israel, and I held deeply critical views of the Israeli government's annexation of occupied territories and its treatment of Palestinians. I worried that the radical/progressive edge of Judaism in the United States was eroding, only to be replaced by a right-wing, anti-Palestinian, pro-Israel-at-all-costs ideology. Once I had decided to spend some of my sabbatical time in Israel, I asked friends to arrange visits to the occupied territories, the "wall," the women's prison, the Bedouin communities, and to set up dinners with Palestinian activists and scholars.

December 2006: He was playing with his grandson, trying to distract the young boy from the stares of the soldiers, the humiliation of the long hot lines, when he caught my eye.

"You're American, no? Jewish? Please tell them what we have to go through just to get home." We had been driving along the contours of the Separation Barrier designed to prevent the "uncontrolled entry of Palestinians into Israel." Our guide works at B'T Selem: The Israel Information Center for Human Rights in the Occupied Palestinian Territories (OPT) (see btselem.org). B'T Selem documents and litigates human rights violations in the OPT. We were joined by a woman who has long been a member of Checkpoint Watch (CPW), a group of

Israeli Jewish women who monitor the checkpoints for human rights violations.

He was an older man, in a long line of men, women, and children, waiting simply to go home, at the Qalandiya checkpoint in Palestine. I stood there, obviously Jewish, for we could move through unencumbered. I remembered a Palestinian scholar, who had spoken only the week before at CUNY, reported dozens and dozens of births at checkpoints, with many infant mortalities and some dead mothers. As we drove to and through these varied checkpoints, I saw the faces of the young soldiers, Jewish men and women probably no more than 19 years old, waving through the Jews and stopping, checking, holding gun to car, to face, to future of the Palestinians who wait, without recourse, as children and grandchildren watch.

Time doesn't seem to matter. At another checkpoint, a friend tells me, a soldier denies two women, traveling together, entry into Israel. A CPW member inquired and learned that the older woman, the aunt, was accompanying her niece, who was supposed to sit for qualifying examinations that afternoon, in order to attend university. The soldier insisted that they lacked the proper papers to be permitted entry. Women from CPW tried to intervene, to no avail. Suddenly, the soldier turned away and the two women ran through.

We'll never know if the soldier turned by intent, if the young woman made it to the exams, if she and her aunt made it home. All we know is that the young woman, her aunt, the soldier, and those who watched were captured and gravely wounded. Obviously and painfully some pay a greater price for injustice. But no one is simply a witness, a bystander. Incidents of intimate state violence ensnare us all; at once joined we also separate. Together traumatized, we split. And only some could drive home. We have an obligation to write at these hyphens of state violence, containment, and what feels like "freedom." Even or especially those of us who can drive away.

CIRCLING BACK

These scenes of my work represent a commitment ignited early in my biography—to embrace the folds in my own skin and the touchpoints where my skin, desires, pain grow intimate with others'; to tell, re-tell, and trouble already settled stories, from a critical perspective of those who have paid the greatest price for "normalized" injustice; to seek out those spaces where the light doesn't shine; to document the long shadow of exclusion and humiliation cast by national policies designed to protect "us," and to ask who is (and is not) "us." And to engage this work as critical, public science.

As the girl child who learned intimately to be repulsed by any mention of pain or loss or sadness as a stain on our family's narrative of prosperity and mobility, I want you to muse about the existential, theoretical, political, and ethical weight of your work as researchers. My plea is that you place your body, your work, your teaching, and your activism squarely inside the opening of the door on Summit Street, on the barbed wire around Bedford Hills prison, at the checkpoint in Palestine, understanding that these hyphenated spaces separate and connect, repulse and ignite, signify oppression and potentiate possibilities unseen. And then you may know to whom your research is accountable (see Fine, 2012; Fine & Torre, 2004; Fine, Weis, Wong, & Weseen, 2000).

CHAPTER 2

Exiles Within

Wild Tongues and Critical Bifocals at the Radical Margins

One of the radical promises of critical research is the possibility that we can tell a different story. As Arundhati Roy (2003) described, in "Confronting Empire," to an audience in Porto Alegre:

> Our strategy should be not only to confront empire, but to lay siege to it. To deprive it of oxygen. To shame it. To mock it. With our art, our music, our literature, our stubbornness, our joy, our brilliance, our sheer relentlessness—and our ability to tell our own stories. Stories that are different from the ones we're being brainwashed to believe.

For more than three decades I have been most fortunate to accompany young people who have been "exiled within" the United States, trying to tell a different story collectively about the histories, structures, and strategies by which young people navigate, laugh, grow angry or sullen, and also resist those forces that expel them from "home," even painful homes. Edward Said (2012) emphasizes that "exile is strangely compelling to think about but terrible to experience. It is the unhealable rift forced between a human being and a native place, between the self and its true home: its essential sadness can never be surmounted" (p. 137).

When reflecting on exile, Said was referencing, of course, occupation and forced exile from Palestine. I borrow his words, like an old sweater, to recast young people of color, and poverty, young LGBTQ/GNC youth, Muslims, immigrants and indigenous, as *exiled within*, from neighborhoods and schools, from streets and the economy, from homes and the national narrative of what it means to belong.

The critical slant of young people situated at the structural rim has focused my collaborative research and writing to theorize their knowledges and wisdom, as they look back critically on dominant arrangements, and look forward to imagine what might be. With ethnographic, and, more recently, participatory methods, we have catalogued insights/incites of despair and wisdom as expressed/embodied by school pushouts, young women in prison, Muslim American youth contending with the U.S. war on terror, children attending profoundly under-resourced and structurally violent schools, and, most recently, LGBTQ youth of color. These young people speak with rage and desire—what Gloria Anzaldúa (1987) would call "wild tongues." With wild tongues and broken hearts, they embody and enact what Sara Ahmed (2014) calls "willful subjects," as a strategy to avoid "extinction."

CRITICAL BIFOCALITY:
SITUATING LIVES IN HISTORICAL AND STRUCTURAL ANALYSIS

After years of research on/with/alongside/by "marginalized youth," I now know it is not enough to gather or document the brilliant "voices" of Black and Latino school pushouts speaking truths about racism and political economy; Muslim Americans calling out Islamophobia; queer youth narrating with exquisite clarity and "radical wit" the deep cuts of heteronormativity in schools, homes, foster care, homeless shelters, policing, and in the intimate space of "home." Once critical researchers chronicle the scar tissue and desires of those who have been shut out, we carry the responsibility to theorize, historicize, make visible, re-present, and re-circulate their stories in the courts, in policy, textbooks, classrooms, curriculum, organizing, and popular media. And we are obligated to animate the histories, structures, policies, ideologies, and practices that have spawned their social exclusion, and perhaps have fomented their deep commitments to justice. "Voices" alone will not suffice. Critical researchers are neither tape recorders nor ventriloquists. And so what do we do with these luscious transcripts scattered around our living room floors?

Lois Weis and I have argued for *critical bifocality* as a theory/method for critical researchers engaged with youth studies:

> We introduce a call for critical bifocality as a way to think about epistemology, design, and the politics of . . . research, as a theory of method in which researchers try to make visible the sinewy linkages or circuits

through which structural conditions are enacted in policy and institutions, as well as the ways in which such conditions come to be woven into community relationships and metabolized by individuals. We seek to trace how circuits of dispossession and privilege travel across zip codes and institutions, rerouting resources, opportunities, and human rights upward as if deserved and depositing despair in low-income communities of color. (Weis & Fine, 2012, p. 173)

Put simply, we call for critical youth studies that place lives in historic and structural contexts. We map young subjectivities within detailed landscapes of opportunities and ideologies, history and policy, cataloguing the stubborn particulars of what Cedric Robinson (1993) would call "racial capitalism" as the soil within which young people make sense, stitch relationships, build lives, organize, resist, conform, and animate rage, despair, and sometimes hope (see also McKittrick, 2006; Melamed, 2011).

In this chapter, critical bifocality offers a lens on the complex subjectivities of two groups of young people who have been exiled within: school pushouts exiting oppressive school contexts with a thirst for educational possibility, and Muslim American youth challenging Islamophobia with righteous pride in religion (Islam) and nation (United States). The pushout narratives contest schools that are underfunded and that are de-skilling students, an economy in which unskilled labor is disposable, and policing practices that place young people at risk of death and incarceration. Muslim American youth mourn for a nation in which they were once embraced and challenge a culture that has stirred up Islamophobia to justify wars far away that enable the taking of oil in the name of "democracy." These young people are of course "voices at the margins," who speak eloquently about the false promises of mobility myths and melting-pot metaphors. They reveal the embodied markings of structural betrayal and alienation. Critics of dominant institutions and ideologies, these young people seek recognition, not assimilation; humanity, not containment. They are exquisite social researchers and analysts, for they see what those of us blinded by "integration" and acceptance often fail to acknowledge. (See Cross, 2003; King, 2015; Ladson-Billings, 2006, 2011; Smith, 2005, for other projects with and about young people of color infused with critical race and Indigenous theory/method, designed so that they might display their critiques, gifts, wounds, activisms, and desires.)

EXILED FROM SCHOOL: RE-FRAMING DROPOUTS

In the mid 1980s, I spent a year going to high school again. I hung out in classrooms at a building I originally called Comprehensive High School (CHS), and then visited school "dropouts" in apartments, parks, and subways, transcribing their full-bodied critiques of schooling, racism, and boredom, and being moved by the yearning for recognition that fueled their early exit from high school. I wrote an ethnographic volume called *Framing Dropouts* (Fine, 1991), in conversation with Paul Willis's *Learning to Labour* (1977). To be clear, this work was not participatory, but I was working with educational justice groups committed to stemming the loss of Black and Brown bodies from public high school prior to graduation.

Based on my "literature review" of "dropouts," I had expected to find young people who had dropped out to be filled with despair, feeling helpless and depressed. What I found instead, after a year of conducting interviews, varied depending on whether the individuals had left school within the previous 3 months or had left school 3 years earlier. The 40 recent dropouts were chatty, filled with social critique, and a rich sense of future possibility. Mobilized by a braided sense of possibility and betrayal, the young people who had just, within months, exited their schools were eloquent in their criticism of the economy and schools, percolating questions about racism, and brimming with hope and enthusiasm for alternatives. A classic response to "What's next?" was "I am going to move to New Jersey; put my baby Tiffany in Catholic schools; attend for-profit proprietary school and start over." Dreams were vivid, hopes strong. Structural critique fueled personal dreams. For a while.

Then I interviewed 25 long-term dropouts. In the intervening 3 years, they had tried and failed in a series of options to schooling. These interviews were hard, for them and for me. Apartments filled with smoke, crying babies, diapers, unpaid bills ("Can you help me understand this bank statement?"), not enough food and too much despair. Awkward requests for money or help. For these young people, over time, their social critique metastasized to self-blame. When we spoke, they were looking backward with some embarrassment and buckets of regrets. "I shouldn't have played cards in seventh grade." "I should have listened to my third grade teacher." Structural critique evaporated, and they presented as self-blaming subjects who were no longer interested in launching a racialized critique of schools or the economy, hoping desperately for another story for their babies.

After 25 years I had an opportunity to reflect on what I did and didn't know at the time of the original research. As it turns out, I had failed to grasp how deeply the long arm of the criminal justice system was reaching into Black and Latino communities in the 1980s. I browsed the opening chapter of the original volume:

> It was 1988 when I sat in the back of what I called Comprehensive High School's auditorium and cried salty tears of joy and rage. . . . Two hundred and fifty young people walked across the stage with flowers and corsages to cheers and the rapid lights of cameras flickering. Mothers, aunts, fathers, siblings, grandparents gathered from the Bronx and Harlem, Puerto Rico, and the Dominican Republic to celebrate their babies graduating high school. My field notes read, "I just want a moment of silence for the five hundred missing." In a school of three thousand, barely one-twelfth graduated. Where are the "disappeared"? If this were a school with middle-class White students, everyone would be outraged; it would be closed. What we tolerate for the poor would be unthinkable for elites. (Fine, 1991, p. 1)

At this school, in the 1980s and certainly since, I learned that it was normative for Black and Brown bodies to drain out of public institutions without diplomas and without setting off alarms. Progressives and conservatives may explain the leakage differently—racism/capitalism versus poor motivation/inadequate intelligence/bad mothering—but too many agreed that it is inevitable.

Moving Black and Brown Bodies from Schools to Prisons

Little did I know that in the late 1980s mass incarceration was seeping aggressively into the darkest neighborhoods of New York State. The state coffers were quietly realigning budgets and transferring monies and bodies of color from schools to prisons. In 1973 the state's prison population was 10,000; by 1980 it had doubled to 20,000; by 1992 it had more than tripled again to almost 62,000 (see Davis, 2003). As I sat in that gymnasium, I didn't realize that the state had other bids on their bodies. Only later would I learn that "since 1989, there have been more blacks entering the prison system for drug offenses each year than there were graduating from SUNY with undergraduate, master's and doctoral degrees—combined" (Gangi, Schiraldi, & Ziedenberg, 1998, p. 7)

Critical bifocality challenges our "epistemologies of ignorance" (Mills, 2012), insisting that we situate the "problem" of school dropouts/pushouts/leavers within a classed and racialized historic matrix of deindustrialization, criminalization, over-policing, underemployment, and gentrification. And then theorize the rich subjectivities narrated by the youth, making legible their embodied wounds and tactics of "survivance" (Vizenor, 1994). Sitting within these structural intersections, these young people could smell the circling smoke of betrayal, even if they couldn't name the forces outside the building pressing for their early exit from school. While the young people couldn't see much beyond their own circumstances and school, I too was limited in the scope of my analysis. My ethnographic eyes kept me searching for the story within the school, looking for the bastard who was tossing Black and Brown bodies out the school doors, but I too needed to see beyond the institutional borders to theorize how racial and class realignments were penetrating schools, hollowing the communities, redesigning the finances, and reassigning racialized bodies to the state prison system.

Patterns of Gentrification and School Closings

Almost 25 years after I first "hung out" at CHS, after generations of disinvestment and disproportionate placement of overage, under-credited students into the building, in the midst of a swelling inequality gap in wealth, income, real estate, and human (in)security, the *New York Times* reported that the school was in "crisis"; it had been declared a failure and it needed to be closed (Hernandez, 2009). Truth was, the neighborhood was gentrifying and the White neighbors wanted their school back (see Lipman, 2011).

Based on test scores, graduation rates, and cumulative disregard, CHS—now acknowledged as Brandeis High School—like so many other comprehensive high schools serving Black and Latino youth, would be closed and re-opened as a complex of four small schools, including the new Frank McCourt High School for Journalism and Writing, sponsored by Symphony Space and adorned with the support of local parents and community. Ironically, given the political commitments of its namesake, the Frank McCourt School was being designed, by some, for the newly gentrifying families of the Upper West Side. The updated ethnography continues, after a quarter-century. I started attending community meetings about the Frank McCourt School. Most of the sessions were cordial and seasoned with public commitments to "diversity." But the slippery discourse of classed and racialized deservingness was leaking through the doors.

"I guess this school will be for 3s and 4s?" asked a White mother, referencing test score signifiers (1–4, with 4 being the highest) burned into the consciousness and identity of New York City youth.

"If we are serious about getting these kinds of students into that building, we'll have to remove the metal detectors," explained another parent, an African American dad in a business suit.

A well-known educational consultant facilitating the discussion elaborated, "If the other schools want to keep the metal detectors, or need them, we might want to use a different entrance." And soon the discursive architecture of separate and unequal was flooding the room, being spoken by White and Black prospective parents who seemed to be among the new gentrifiers:

> The building will be open to children citywide, using criteria that are demographically neutral. Only those students who satisfy the published criteria—score a 3 or 4 on standardized tests, submit a writing sample in English, have good attendance, and post a grade point average of 3.0 in middle school—need apply, and have their parents submit their names into a lottery.

Standardized test scores are highly correlated with race and class; privately paid tutors often coach writing samples in English, and steady attendance and high GPA are, of course, associated with stable housing. Lotteries systematically under-enroll very poor families, English language learners, and special education students. And yet this strategy of educational reform mislabeled "choice" ends up segregating children by race/ethnicity, class, and academic history into varying strata of schools; measuring and publicizing stratified outcome data; declaring crisis and closing schools and reopening them for more selective public school students and/or corporate charter students (Fabricant & Fine, 2012, 2013; see Fine & Ruglis, 2009, on circuits of dispossession).

In November 1903, W. E. B. Du Bois published the first issue of _The Crisis: A Record of the Darker Races_, insisting that a record be kept of the ongoing crisis of "the darker races." Du Bois recognized that crisis, for poor people and Blacks in the United States, had been woven deeply into the fabric of our nation's history (see Du Bois, 1899). Most significant for our purposes, Du Bois noted that the structural and historic educational crises of the "darker races" would be routinely ignored until there was a profit to be made. Today, as we hear the calls of "crisis," and celebrations of neighborhood revitalization, the wise ghost of Du Bois asks us to be suspicious.

Re-Placing Lives in Racialized Histories

When I launched the original project at Brandeis I was committed to researching the "dropout" crisis in the context of educational history, critical race theory, and political economy. As a White researcher not from the community, however, I had little idea that racialized mass incarceration was beginning to channel Black and Brown bodies from schools into prisons. Had the project been participatory, clearly community-based activists and researchers would have insisted that we interrogate these structural links between schools and prisons, even in the 1980s. When I returned to the building, a quarter of a century later, my map of institutional networks engorged, I learned about the deep entanglements of educational "reform" with policing and prisons, the highly profitable testing industry, the Whitening of neighborhoods through gentrification. I understood what Jessica Ruglis and I later called "circuits of dispossession" (Fine & Ruglis, 2009).

In the 1980s, truth be told, I probably thought I was conducting a study of "dropouts" to "give them voice." I know now that is not only intellectually anemic and politically problematic, it's just bad research. A simple study of "dropouts" must be situated within these deeply racialized and classed circuits of policy and economy, moving bodies, opportunities, and money in ways that dispossess the most marginalized young people in New York City and privilege the children of elites. And the soul of the research must be the perspectives of those who have been pushed out, but these "voices" must float in an intellectually and politically rich sea of critical analysis. Schools are public institutions deeply nested in the housing-economy-education-criminal justice matrix. As new and newer "reforms" take shape, youth of color and poverty dangle in the political winds, their bodies and educations expendable to market forces, as corporate influence saturates the public project of public education and gentrification surrounds. These young people sense the grinding gears around them, and it is the job of research—preferably participatory—to narrate how lives navigate the oppressive systems we can see, and more important, those we can't. And how narratives of "progress" blanket the disrupted lives and communities left behind.

Public policies that facilitate dispossession through racialized and classed disinvestment and through what is called "restructuring" are instituted as if historically innocent and demographically neutral. They are "transparent" only in the sense that we can't really see them, but they are everywhere. In the 1980s young people at the margins knew they were being silenced; their bodies refused to be "pushed out," so they ironically "dropped out," refusing extinction. But they knew, even if they couldn't narrate, that they were holding education seats warm until the "deserving" students could arrive. This kind of theoretical project represents the pulse of critical bifocality, refusing to cauterize outcomes from processes of dispossession and relentlessly tracing how ghosts, histories, and structures penetrate subjectivities (see Foucault, 1977; Gordon, 1997).

EXILED FROM HOME: WHEN MUSLIM AMERICAN YOUTH LEARNED THEY DIDN'T "BELONG"

If school dropouts, or pushouts, come to feel as if they don't "belong" in schools and leave through a process of slow violence, Muslim American young people in the United States learned quickly right after 9/11 that they didn't "belong" to the only nation they considered home (Abu El Haj, 2015; Arshad, 2016).

In 2004, Selcuk Sirin and I facilitated a series of focus groups with Muslim American youth, mostly middle- and upper-middle-class U.S. citizens, who lived comfortably in the suburbs of New York City until the towers fell and their classmates and educators began to suspect, maybe, that the boys were terrorists and the girls were oppressed. Sirin, a professor of psychology at New York University, asked me to join him on a project to document how Muslim American youth development fractured into what we called hyphenated selves once they were exiled from the moral community called "America" (Sirin & Fine, 2007, 2008).

At the time there were somewhere between three and seven million Muslims (an estimate; the U.S. Census does not track religious affiliation) in the United States, approximately two-thirds of whom were immigrants. With the "war on terror" abroad and at home, these young people were ideologically banished from the only moral community they knew. Like Japanese Americans sent to internment camps in California in the 1940s, Muslim American youth learned, in 2001, that their citizen status in the United States was provisional. They had grown suspect while sitting still.

Initial Study, 2004

Three years after 9/11, Selcuk and I set out to conduct a small partic-ipatory project with mostly middle- and upper-middle-class Muslim youth in New Jersey. We expected to find a cohort of somewhat intim-idated young people feeling vulnerable to government surveillance, ambivalent about religion, highly conflicted about national identities, with some perhaps trying to pass. We expected to find a rising anti–U.S. sentiment. But we were wrong, at least then.

Identity Maps. To design the research we gathered a small, diverse advisory group comprised of Muslim American youth aged 12–25 to help us shape the research questions, methods, and analysis. To be-gin, we facilitated focus groups of Muslim youth asking them to draw maps of "your many identities." While the drawings were often stun-ning, detailed, and firmly rooted in Islam, three "forms" emerged. Some young people explained that they were in both "worlds," re-fusing to consider their "American" self and their "Muslim" self to be in conflict. As Figure 2.1 suggests, a full 61%, particularly young women, thrilled at the blended possibilities of being Muslim and American.

Tahani, a 17-year-old Syrian American, explained how she justi-fies wearing a hijab to inquisitive Americans in her high school and on the streets: "I tell people wearing a scarf is like wearing a bicycle hel-met; it protects me and gives me courage to travel where I fear." And when Hadice, 16, was asked how she feels when classroom discussions about war and terrorism turn awkwardly her way, she sighed: "Well, I educate them. Really, if I don't, who will? Who better than me, I watch Al-Jazeera, FOX, CNN news—my peers just go to the mall. So it's my job to educate them." Shira, whose map is shown in Figure 2.2, voiced a similar sentiment of moving between cultures with relative ease, while fielding many intrusive questions.

A few of the participants sketched what may be thought of as "parallel" lives, negotiating across two distinct but separated worlds. Narib, as you can see in Figure 2.3, hangs in the space between his two countries, dangling from a question mark. And yet some (11%), even as early as 2004, represented a deep, embodied fracture of the soul, as Amir portrayed in his "map" called Tears for Racism (see

**Figure 2.1.
Blended Lines**

**Figure 2.2.
Flower of Identities**

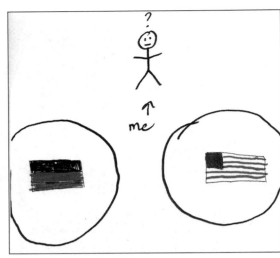

**Figure 2.3.
Dangling Between**

**Figure 2.4.
Tears for Racism**

**Figure 2.5.
Cracked Globe**

Figure 2.4), or as Waled reveals in the image of a fractured world in Figure 2.5.

Survey Data. Turning to the quantitative survey data from 2004, we gathered information from 70 teens (aged 12–18), from a range of Arab and Muslim nationalities, with 84% born in the United States. We also surveyed 97 young adults (aged 18–25), with 46% born in the United States, with backgrounds from an equally wide range of Middle Eastern, Asian, and some Northern African countries. From the combined samples, 84% reported that they had experienced discrimination in the last 6 months due to their religion, but almost none had told their families or, of course, the police. In terms of ethnic and national identities (clunky items that proved more useful, however), most youth rated themselves as "highly Muslim" and "highly American"—there was no "clash" in their cultures. Yet early signs of alienation were present in the data. Those young people who reported high levels of Islamophobic discrimination also reported feeling more depression, anxiety, and physical signs of illness than their Muslim American peers who reported lower levels of discrimination. They rated themselves as less "American," less engaged, and more alienated. When they encountered a discriminatory comment or person, their responses varied in important ways:

- 35% said they "educate others"
- 22% challenge the stereotypes on the spot
- 13% respond with exasperated rejoinders like "We are normal Americans!"
- 11% said that they struggle, internally, with how to respond

Males in particular worried that any response would render them the "angry Muslim" who could be misread as dangerous. We note, then, the devastating psychological, physical, social, and political consequences of discrimination, exclusion, and state-sponsored exile.

There is a tragic irony in the belief that more discrimination against and exclusion of any Othered group keeps the rest of "us" safe. To the contrary, our evidence suggests that the more discrimination and exclusion young people experience, the more they feel alienated, disconnected, and disengaged. Then no one is "safe."

Responses of Youth. Counter to our early expectations, through identity maps, surveys, focus groups, and interviews, we "met" a group of Muslim American youth who are (of course!) a hugely diverse and dignified group of young people. All shared the simple fact that the war on terror, in the Middle East and in the United States, had indeed fully altered their lives, penetrating their sense of themselves here and there. Flung from the comfort of inclusion within the "American" middle class, they were suddenly branded as Other at home. These political ruptures cut into the skin—no one was immune. But their responses to these forms of political violence varied enormously.

With great diversity, these young people voiced both critique of what they called "America," and a full-bodied sense of themselves as "American." Most narrated a right and desire to belong, a relentless sense of entitlement to be viewed as a patriot, a "real American," like their Japanese American peers had done 50 years before. Neither hiding nor filled with shame, they asserted a Muslim American identity stitched, precariously, into the national fabric. Sometimes they self-described as patriotic, some as angry or conflicted, never as terrorist, and very often as dissenting citizens. Most were willing to educate others who displayed Islamophobic ignorance. And many, since, have linked arms with various social justice movements, including Black Lives Matter, undocumented-student struggles, LGBTQ youth organized against aggressive policing, and/or censorship on college campuses. From the drip feed of structural and intimate violence and exclusion emerge subjectivities of determination and in many cases solidarities with "Others" under siege.

Follow-Up Study, 2016–2017

More than a decade has passed since that initial study. Islamophobic speech, hate crimes, and official mandates from the President of the United States have spiked. The young people coming of age have not been *exiled* from the moral community in which they thought they belonged. Instead, they have *grown up* in a sea of Islamophobia. And under the Trump presidency, their fears as immigrants, and as Muslims, have dramatically and legitimately swelled.

Recently I presented the data to a gathering of 300 Muslim and Arab students at Queensborough Community College, in New York City, on the severe rise in Islamophobic hate crimes (see Center for the Study of Hate and Extremism, 2016). I asked for a show of hands if they had recently experienced "more" discriminatory treatment in public spaces, streets, malls, on campus, and in subways. Most hands went up. "Why?" "Trump!" "ISIS!" "The media!"

Then I asked, "How many of you told your parents?" No hands. "The police?" No hands. "A teacher?" No hands. "My mother won't let me go to college—or go out—if I tell her what happens." "My brother, Mohammed, died in the World Trade Towers; he had a Muslim name. For months they were accusing him of being a terrorist rather than supporting us as a grieving family. We don't ask for help anymore." "My aunt won't take her children to the Emergency Room if they fall because she is afraid she will be deported." These young people are contending alone with cumulative verbal and social threats to their identity, suspicion and scrutiny, questions that challenge their "belonging" in the only country (for most) they have ever known. And they tell virtually no one.

In a generation, the buoyant—almost naïve—sense of hybridity, possibility, and "integration" that we heard in 2004 is curdling. Today, we hear far more alienation; fear of public authorities; suspicion of words like *democracy, equality,* or *justice* coming from the government; far less interest in "educating" other Americans. Even more than in 2004, casual behaviors—hanging out, going to parks, walking down the street, laughing aloud with friends, talking on a cellphone in Arabic, sending money home—are scrutinized. The Internet is monitored; campuses have been infiltrated by police departments, and young people are watched—as are their parents. African American and Latino youth have long read these messages "between the lines" of American democracy talk. Now Muslim American youth are joining the ranks of "dissenting citizens" (Maira, 2004).

And yet today we also bear witness as calls for interfaith dialogue multiply; as Muslim American students join on-campus coalitions with Black Lives Matter, undocumented students, and LGBTQ groups, and mobilize with Black and Latino youth, undocumented youth, and LGBTQ youth against aggressive policing, for immigration justice and human rights. This is a bipolar political moment, in which there is collective protest and public cataloguing of microaggressions and spiked enactments of state and social violence. While some retreat and others dig deeply into their own Muslim American communities and organizations, many are (also) coming out of the shadows and embracing cross-group campaigns for social justice as political solidarities flourish.

CRITICAL BIFOCALITY AS THEORY-METHOD

Critical bifocality, introduced earlier in this chapter, enables us to theorize with young people about the current instance of a long and painful legacy of Othering that characterizes U.S. history. Shifting groups of youth—tagged as "Other" depending on the national enemy du jour (Native, Black, Mexican American, Japanese American, Muslim, immigrant, queer, trans . . .)—embody and enact the social and psychological dynamics of being exiled within (see Harris, 1993; Pruitt, 2004; Sullivan & Tuana, 2007, on how Whiteness remains the "unnamed" subject). They narrate their own lives but, as important, they refract back on the shape and policies of a nation designed, and regularly refashioned, to exclude.

Young people who have cultivated wisdom at the margins of institutional betrayal and economic/racial/sexuality oppression know well the embodiments of and survival skills honed in precarious circumstances. They anticipate with exquisite precision (some might mistakenly call it paranoia) the evil woven into the shadowed underbelly of our public and private institutions, and they narrate with humor and enact with care the individual and collective habits necessary to survive and reimagine what else is possible. As bell hooks (1989) has written:

> marginality is much more than a site of deprivation, in fact . . . it is also the site of radical possibility, a space of resistance. It was this marginality that I was naming as a central location for the production of a counterhegemonic discourse that is not just found in words but in habits of being and the way one lives. (p. 206)

Across contexts, deeply marginalized young people are exquisitely aware of how intimate, cultural, and institutional settings expunge, punish, repel, and fetishize their "differences," such that devastating economic, educational, violent, and psychic assaults accumulate—not for all, but for many—and they are equally strategic about finding and offering care to those thrown to the wind. Whereas dropouts were "produced" as disposable by a linked series of historic and structural circumstances, and Muslim Americans were appropriated as the deflecting Other to justify a war for oil, we can nevertheless hear their committed and embodied expressions of "difference," their "willful subjects" (Ahmed, 2014), and their demands for justice narrated at the radical margins.

It would be a mistake, and an act of epistemological violence, to study these young people as simply depressed and giving up, or hostile to the nation. They are building selves of integrity as they metabolize the paper cuts of deportation at home. Our work as researchers is to refuse the colonial gaze that seeks pathology or imminent terror in their bodies; our task is to attach the affects and wisdom to the history and structures in which their lives are situated. Leigh Patel (2016) writes,

> I do not concede that the pursuit of knowledge is doomed to colonial referents. In fact regarding research as fundamentally a relational endeavor of seeking and communicating knowledge opens up materially transformative inquiries into the coordinates used. . . . I frame research as a permeable and relational force . . . destabilize[ing] overly linear conceptualizations of cause, effect, objectivity and implications while also not shirking responsibility. (p. 48)

Critical bifocality is a provisional design strategy to re-place in history and context and to theorize with those who best know the keloids of oppression, the deeply social psychological fabric of contemporary injustice, taking up the difficult theoretical and empirical work of tracing circuited flows of capital, bodies, ideas, affects, subjectivities, and power, refracting the dominant story (see Katz, 2003, on counter-topography). Students who appear to be giving up on education are resituated as complex actors laboring at the structural intersection of a disinvested education system, a shrinking labor market, an unjust criminal justice system, and a gentrifying urban housing market. Muslim American youth navigating violence in their native countries and surveillance in the United States narrate the psychological labors of negotiating hyphenated selves, in a lineage with Japanese American youth 50 years prior, revealing the strategic subjectivities deployed when a nation called "home" exiles them from within. Careful narrators of their own lives, they are exquisitely positioned analysts of a nation that markets democracy, freedom, and justice.

CHAPTER 3

Civics Lessons
The Color and Class of Educational Betrayal and Desire

with April Burns, María Elena Torre, and Yasser A. Payne

Every day, every hour, talented students are being sacrificed. . . . They're [the schools] destroying lives.

—Maritza, college student, speaking about her urban high school

Obviously there's no there's . . . there are not enough books [and] there's overcrowding . . . I'm expected to teach a class of forty-eight to forty-six students with only thirty-six books with only thirty-six chairs. If those conditions don't improve, education can't improve. Again, go to any other school—and of course you're going to see better academic programs because [there are] more resources for more children, more one on one interactions with student to teacher. And again, I'm only one person. I don't have a TA. I don't have any assistance in the classroom except the other kids. . . . Overcrowding . . . we're expected to perform miracles, part a Red Sea, if you will.

—Joel Vaca, educator

In 2002 I (Michelle) was invited to participate in a class action suit lodged by low-income immigrant and youth of color attending profoundly under-resourced schools in California. The conditions so normalized at Brandeis in the East were now being contested in high schools in the West. I invited April Burns, Yasser Payne, and María Torre to join the legal research team, and we agreed to gather stories from young people about their educational experiences and desires. The task was to place their stories in the history of educational policy and institutional dynamics, and then draft an evidence-rich story

29

to tell in court about the devastating cost of racialized miseducation. Presented here is a slightly revised version of our expert report. This chapter (Fine, Burns, Payne, & Torre, 2004) was produced after a year of research in resource-starved schools in California, invited by lawyers and families who had faith that their stories might inspire a small step toward justice in schools.

In so many buildings we call public schools, the spirits of poor and working-class urban youth of color and their educators are assaulted in ways that bear academic, psychological, social, economic, and perhaps, also, criminal justice consequences. We write on the devastation wrought by *alienating public schools* (Delpit, 1993; Woodson, 2000). Theorizing within and beyond reproduction theory (Anyon, 2005; Bowles & Gintis, 1976), we seek to understand the psychological and social devastation incited by buildings that are structurally damaged, educators who are undercredentialed, institutions with neither intellectually nor politically enticing projects for youth to undertake (cf. Bowles & Gintis, 1976; Cross, 2003; Darling-Hammond, 2010; King & Swartz, 2014; Ladson-Billings, 2011; Oakes, 1988; Valenzuela, 1999).

This chapter seeks to expose not simply the material conditions that poor and working-class students contend with in their schools, and not simply the testing regimes that injure the spirit of teaching and learning. Instead, we venture in this essay to study how *class consciousness* comes to be inscribed on and embodied by poor and working-class youth, through their schools. While we have no illusions that schools alone convey these insidious messages or that schools alone could dismantle the gross racial and class inequities that characterize our nation (see Anyon, 2005), we do know that schools—as a public institution—whisper intimately the words that land on and saturate the souls of youth.

As an expert witness, I was invited into the *Williams v. California* lawsuit, brought by a class of California youth attending severely under-resourced schools. We report here on focus group and survey material we gathered from more than 100 students and graduates of these schools, about the conditions of their schools and the consequences. The data are compelling on a simple point: Schools are public institutions that convey unequivocally to poor children and youth their fundamental disposability.

In these places we call schools, poor and working-class youth, oftentimes immigrants, come to see how class fundamentally organizes our nation, how hollow the promise of meritocracy is, how vast and enduring social inequities are, and how written off they and their peers have become.

As the public sphere realigns so that state dollars increasingly finance prisons and military recruiters, testing industries and zero-tolerance measures in schools, poor and working-class youth of color are *reading* these conditions of their schools as evidence of public betrayal. Not simply incorporating the messages, these girls and boys/ young women and men critically analyze social arrangements of class and race stratification and their "place" in the social hierarchy. Like children who learn to love in homes scarred by violence, they are being asked to learn in contexts of humiliation, betrayal, and disrespect. It would be inaccurate to say that youth are learning nothing in urban schools of concentrated poverty. Neither fully internalizing this evidence nor fully resisting it, these children are learning their perceived worth in the social hierarchy. This profound civics lesson may well burn a hole in their collective souls.

In the early part of the 21st century, schools of poverty and alienation transform engaged and enthused youth into young women and men who believe that the nation, adults, and the public sphere have abandoned and betrayed them, in the denial of quality education, democracy, the promise of equality. Were that not enough, California marks the "cutting edge state" in which historic commitments to affirmative action in higher education have been retrenched, wrenching even dreams of college and university out of the imaginations of generations of African Americans and Latinos. Youth know that the blades of race, class, and ethnicity cut the cloth of public resources, to determine who receives, and who is denied, a rich public education.

Many have written eloquently on this perverse realignment of the public sphere to satisfy and engorge elite interests—that is, to gentrify the public sphere. But few have interrogated how poor and working-class youth of color witness, analyze, critique, and mobilize in the face of this state realignment. This is the project we ended up documenting —the critical class consciousness of American youth, specifically how they view material injustices, procedural injustices, and what Nancy Fraser (1995) calls the (in)justice of being denied recognition.

We take the California schools in question to be emblematic of a growing set of public schools, located in communities of poverty and communities of color, increasingly segregated and obsessed with testing and classification, in which facilities are in desperate disrepair, faculty are undercredentialed and turning over at alarming rates, and instructional materials are fully inadequate to the task of educating for rigor and democracy. These schools are not simply reproducing race and class inequities. Far worse, these schools educate poor and working-class youth, and youth of color, away from academic mastery and democracy, toward academic ignorance and civic alienation.

LEARNING FROM THOSE WHO ENDURE:
THE DYNAMICS OF THE FOCUS GROUPS

To prepare our expert report, we collected data from a broad range of students attending schools in the "plaintiff class." Jury research firms were hired to conduct random-digit dialing in affected neighborhoods in order to generate the survey and focus group samples. Four criteria were specified: respondents needed to be current students, not dropouts; respondents needed to be reached via random-digit dialing (no friendship or snowball nominations); respondents could not be connected to, or made explicitly aware of, the litigation until after the interview; and parental consent was essential. Approximately 400 calls were placed to generate each focus group of 10 to 12 young adults. Interviewed students were educational "survivors" (not dropouts), randomly identified, and not selected from within peer or friendship patterns.

A multimethod research design was undertaken: *surveys* were completed anonymously by 86 middle- and high-school focus group members, prior to their involvement in the focus group discussion; 11 *focus groups* were facilitated with 101 youth attending plaintiff schools in the San Francisco, Oakland, and Los Angeles areas, as well as a group (of peers) in Watsonville; and 11 *telephone interviews* were held with graduates of California schools that fall within the plaintiff class. All of these graduates are currently in attendance at college.

Survey-based gender and race/ethnicity data on 86 students indicate: 44 females and 42 males; 4 students who identify as White, 1 Biracial, 25 Latino/Hispanic, and 56 Black. Parental and student consent were obtained for all focus group participants. In a few cases in which there was no parental consent, participants were turned away.

CUMULATIVE INEQUITY: SCHOOLING TOWARD ALIENATION

Counter to the stereotype that poor youth don't care about education, the youth whom we interviewed were clear and insistent: They want high-quality, demanding teachers. They are upset when such teachers leave their schools midyear or after just one year, which is typical. The evidence from elementary, middle, high school, and college students —cross-sectional for sure—reveals, over time, how yearning for quality educators warps to anger about denied access to such educators; how pride in self curdles to shame in miseducation; and how local civic engagement shrinks away from national commitments to citizenship. These three institutional dynamics are central to this production of *schooling toward alienation*.

The longer students stay in schools with structural problems, high levels of uncertified teachers, high teacher turnover, and inadequate instructional materials, the wider the academic gaps between White children and children of color, or wealthy children and poor children, grow to be, and the more alienated the students become (Anand, Fine, Perkins, Surrey, & the Renaissance Graduating Class of 2000, 2002; Bryk & Schneider, 2003; Delpit, 1993; Fine, 1991; Noguera, 2003; Oakes, 1988; Pruitt, 2000/2011; Valenzuela, 1999). Schools of alienation cumulatively incite a process that warps yearning into anger, pride into shame, and local engagement into civic alienation (Fine & Ruglis, 2009).

From Yearning to Anger

> Right now I have this one teacher that's like, he's my English teacher and he's like really trying to help the students right now. We're looking into colleges and stuff. He's really trying to help us, like learn things, because it's like, he'll pull you out of class for a reason. It will be like to learn the stuff.
>
> —High school girl

These students know what good education looks like. And they want it. Across focus groups and surveys, the students were very clear that they want teachers who care and who demand rigorous work. We asked the students, "What does a teacher who cares look like?" Students described a "good" teacher as someone who holds high standards and helps students reach those standards. Someone who listens, asks questions, and listens to student answers. Students were excited about teachers who want to know what students think. Some praised faculty who assign lots of homework, if they provide support and time to finish.

Girl: Like he said, we got a lot of substitutes right now. . . . Some of them cap [put you down], some of them play football. That's not what we come to school for. So we got our teachers there that are pretty cool. But last year we had all our teachers. I love the good teachers, but the best ones are like . . .
Boy: They change the whole school around.
Girl: They change the whole school.
Boy: My favorite is all the good teachers.

These students know the difference between "substitutes" who "play football" and teachers who "change the whole school around." They appreciate a caring teacher who is responsive when they are confused. A good teacher wants to know the students, and provides lots of red marks on their papers. Trouble is, few of these students encounter and enjoy "good" teachers on a regular basis. Most explain that they have had a range of teachers. Too many, however, have disappeared midyear, are long-term substitutes, or don't know their content areas. In the plaintiff schools, the percentage of fully certified teachers ranges from 13–50%. In the State of California, the percentage of undercredentialed teachers in a school is directly related to the percentage of students of color and students eligible for free or reduced-price meals, rising to an average of 24% noncredentialed teachers for 91–100% of students eligible for free or reduced-price lunch. Teacher turnover rates are reported by some principals to be as high as 40% in a matter of 2 to 3 years.

By high school, the yearning for quality educators bumps into the realization, by these youth, that they are being denied. At the bump, resignation blends with anger. The optimism of youth seems to drain by high school, when students describe teachers "only there for a paycheck" or other adults who "know, they know, they just ignorant and don't care about us." By high school, the youth believe that they are being denied a fair share of resources for their education (Fine & Burns, 2003). At this point, the yearning converts to anger:

When I ask for help, and there's too many kids and I know the teacher can't pay attention to me, I'm ignored. That makes me mad. They blame kids when they can't fix things.

The structural conditions of their schools, combined with the belief that White and wealthy youth receive better, provoke a sense of anger voiced by many youth, particularly high school students whom we interviewed. These young women and men express a cumulative and piercing sense of *relative deprivation*; a substantial discrepancy between what they believe they deserve and what they actually receive. Relative deprivation, with associated anger and grievance, derives when individuals experience a discrepancy between what they have and what they want; what they have and what they believe they deserve; what they don't have and others do.

It is important to be clear. It is not the case that these youths simply internalize the messages that the broader society is targeting at them. Nor is it the case that they simply resist these messages. In a complex montage of internalization, resistance, and transformation, these young women and men clearly and unambivalently read their social disposability and their political dispensability. They know they are viewed as unworthy. With the wisdom of "dual consciousness" (Du Bois, 1903), and through the hazy gauze of meritocratic ideology, miseducation, and false promises, with the guillotine blade of high-stakes testing overhead, they speak through dual registers of yearning and anger, pride and shame, engagement and alienation, fear and desire (Woodson, 2000). They can, at once, critique the dominant ideologies about poor kids, urban youth, and pathology, and mimic these same sentiments when asked to evaluate other students who are having difficulties. Perhaps the ultimate sign of their desire to belong, to be citizens with a place at the table, is that they are *critics*, *consumers*, and *producers* of a meritocratic ideology. And they are angry that despite their willingness to engage, they are denied, as one girl explains:

> I'm in tenth grade. And what I like about my school, or what I don't like about my school is how they teach us like animals, like they cage us up and like they keep putting more gates and more locks and stuff and then they expect us to act like humans and I feel like if you treat us like animals that's how we going to act. . . .

In a series of comments that are difficult to hear, the next set of students are concerned that educators "treat us like inmates" or think they are "coming in to teach killers." In the absence of a community of qualified educators and a rich, intellectually engaging school environment, most youth turn away from the academic and relational features of schooling with a blend of anger, resignation, and despair. Those who graduate feel little loyalty to their high schools and, sometimes, even what may sound like survivor guilt.

> Leaving my high school was sad but I didn't do enough at
> [my high school] to make it better. It pains me to see what my
> younger brothers and sisters go through at [my high school]. I
> feel guilty about my opportunities, compared to others in my
> community and seriously considered dropping out of college
> several times. . . . You know, it's hard to know that I am getting
> an education while other people I know aren't. I guess I'm the
> lucky one, given all of the students who couldn't beat the stacked
> odds. (Chantal, graduate, now in college)

The anger bleeds toward some educators, privileged youth from other communities, and the broken promise of democracy for all. Within these statements of anger, however, there is still pride, hope, and a yearning for something to change.

From Pride to Shame

Alongside the anger lays a complex geographic splitting of pride and shame. That is, the students speak with pride about themselves within their local communities, and then mumble quietly, with some shame, as they imagine themselves venturing beyond.

Across the focus groups with current students, and in individual interviews with graduates, the youth spoke with some confidence about self, family, and community. They told us they have "skills" that other youth don't have, developed, largely, through confrontation with adversity. "I think we have more life experience." "We have street knowledge." "We're smarter, we're not just all proper." "We know about struggling, trying to get to the top, and not just, you know, bouncing right up there." Some of these same youth commented upon specific positive aspects of their schools. A number recall fondly teachers who supported them in hard times.

To the extent that students spoke with strength and confidence, they were speaking about their selves *within* their communities. Once they discursively wandered beyond the borders of the local, shame, stigma, and fear peppered their talk. At that point, they describe themselves as academically handicapped by opportunities denied, ill equipped to attend a "real" or "serious" college, embarrassed by limited vocabulary, math skills, and limited exposure to elite culture.

As if characters in Sennett and Cobb's *The Hidden Injuries of Class* (1993), these students spoke of the "lacks" that their education has instilled in them, as if they embodied the inferiority of their schooling. As one young woman told us:

> [If kids from a wealthy school came in here right now,] I wouldn't talk because they would be more sophisticated or something, and understand words I don't know and I don't want to be embarrassed.

Students explain that they have been systematically miseducated because people in government, throughout the state, and even some of their teachers *want* them to be ignorant. One focus group conversation was particularly chilling on this point:

> Yes, that be like putting all the bad kids in one school, that's just like putting, you know, just like putting them in jail. They going to be crazy. . . .

It was painful to listen as some students explained that they believe that schools *want* students to feel ashamed or embarrassed, so that the students will leave and classes will become smaller, with no adult responsibility for the loss of student bodies. These interviews reveal a raw sense of social disposability, and—as penetrating—the students' sense of helplessness to disrupt these conditions (Noguera, 2003; Oakes, 1988; Valenzuela, 1999; Woodson, 2000). Michael Lewis (1992) argues that youth or adults who endure a prolonged experience of shame are likely to express anger, "an emotional substitute for unacknowledged shame . . . a reaction to a frustration of action . . . a reaction to an injury to self" (p. 150).

Contexts of Filth, Disrespect, and Disrepair. Toward the end of each focus group we circled the room, asking each student to suggest one element of their "ideal school." It was striking when a young girl whispered, with some initial hesitation but then elegant simplicity: "If I could have my ideal school, I guess I would have seats on the toilets and enough paper in the bathroom to clean yourself." One young man offered, "If you go to a dirty school, you feel like you're dirty, you know, not clean."

A second form of shame was narrated: the shame of being educated in contexts of filth and decay. Schools, like other contexts of childhood and adolescence, are not simply the places where development happens. They are intimate places where youths construct identities, build a sense of self, read how society views them, develop the capacity to sustain relationships, and forge the skills to initiate change. These are the contexts where youth grow or they shrink. Environmental psychologists Werner and Altman (1998) argue:

> Children are not separate from their actions or feelings, nor are they separate from other children or the physical, social and temporal circumstances that comprise unfolding events. They are so interconnected that one aspect can not be understood without the others. . . . The street . . . is not separate from its inhabitants. (p. 125)

Buildings in disrepair are not, therefore, merely a distraction; they are identity-producing and self-defining. Since the early part of the 20th century, psychologists and sociologists have argued that children and youth develop a sense of self from the messages they gather from adults and peers, structures and institutions, around them. What the culture says about the child, his family, and his community comes to be internalized, in part, by that child. Children who are valued tend to be more positive in self-concept than those who are disparaged. This value may be communicated in what people say about and to them. But just as powerful, the quality of the contexts in which they are growing "speaks" to youth about how they are viewed and valued. If surrounded by decay, disrepair, and filth, and no adult intervening to protect, a child may come to see herself as worthy of little or at least that adults see her as unworthy.

Student Alondra Jones details the corrosive effects of a negative structural context on the developing selves of young students:

> It makes me, you know what, in all honesty, I'm going to break something down to you. It make you feel less about yourself, you know, like you . . . here in a class where you have to stand up because there's not enough chairs and you see rats in the buildings, the bathrooms is nasty, you got to pay. And then you, like I said, I visited Mann Academy, and these students, if they want to sit on the floor, that's because they choose to. And that just makes me feel real less about myself because it's like the State don't care about public schools. If I have to . . . stand in the class, they can't care about me. It's impossible. So in all honesty, it really makes me feel bad about myself.

A number of environmental studies demonstrate the specific psychological and physiological effects of environmental stressors such as crowding, noise, heat, and other structural factors on students' capacity to concentrate and produce academic work. Studies show that these stressors also induce high levels of negative interactions and anger among and within the youth. Robert S. McCord (2002), in a systematic analysis of schools in San Francisco Unified School District concludes,

> The findings of my school facility appraisal reported in this Declaration point to a pattern of disparate facility conditions associated with the racial and ethnic identity of SFUSD schools. This pattern of disparate conditions is likely to convey the message of racial inferiority that is implicit in a policy of segregation. (p. 12)

Valkiria Durán-Narucki (2008) found that structural building quality predicts students' attendance, which, in turn, bears directly on academic achievement. The links are significant. The youth concurred. In one focus group, a series of comments reveals how overcrowding affects learning:

> *Boy:* I just feel like it's deep—right now it's like five thousand people overcrowded. It's way overcrowded. And it's like, you know, you don't even have to go there [inaudible], because basically they don't know if we go there, you can just come on campus or whatever. Like right now, we got three different tracks, and they don't know, like, if you don't have an ID, you just, like, you can tell them you have to take your ID picture or whatever and just go on in, and they'll believe you, because they don't really know who go there, because they've got so many kids in that school.
> *Interviewer:* But how does that affect you as a student?
> *Boy:* Because, like, they could let the wrong person on campus or whatever or, like [inaudible], and it's really too many people, just . . . last year, I had forty-two kids in my algebra class.

Saegert and Winkel (1999) and Krenichyn, Saegert, and Evans (2001) document the psychological and physiological impact of crowding and other environmental stressors on youth. Evans (2004) reviews a massive literature demonstrating the adverse consequences of poverty, and environmental assault on youth, including studies documenting that in the presence of noise youth blood pressure rises, concentration diminishes, and errors on difficult tasks multiply; and that substandard educational building conditions can hurt student performance, accounting for a 5% to 11% reduction of student performance on standardized tests.

These schools not only stress youth and educators. The evidence suggests that they also fail to buffer poor and working-class youth from the stressors they experience outside of school. As Kliewer and Lepore (2015) and others have documented, working and learning in conditions of environmental stress not only undermine the capacity to concentrate and complete difficult tasks, but may compromise students' and educators' abilities to adapt to the many other stressors they do, and will, confront.

Self-Blame and Academic Troubles. Across the focus groups we could hear a fleeting, infrequent, but emotionally powerful discourse of self-blame for past mistakes. While most of these youth attribute their miseducation to structural inequities, a strong undercurrent of student blame pierced the focus groups, as this girl expresses:

> When I was in middle school . . . I skipped that grade, went right to the ninth grade from seventh grade. I chose to mess that ninth grade year up. I chose to cut and shoot dice and be doing other things that I'm not supposed to do, you know. So that was my mistake, my fault. You know, in my tenth grade year, I destroyed it, you know. I made nothing of it all, nothing. I passed, I don't know how I passed, you know. So when I look at my transcript, I look at it and say this is where I failed. I know I won't be able to make it into a university because of me, not because of what peer pressure or what this principal said or what this teacher was teaching me.

While the students discussed, in the aggregate, structural problems of teacher turnover, overcrowding, absence of books, ineffective guidance counselors, and so forth, they also accepted much responsibility for their own behaviors. A whispered discourse flows through the groups, revealing self-blame for past behaviors. Students who offered such analyses typically asserted a very punitive, neoliberal perspective on their own biographies: Past mistakes do and should dictate a life of impoverished educational, social, and economic opportunities.

Students who view educational difficulties as largely their own fault have little sense that school can or will help them achieve positive educational outcomes (Fine et al., 1991). Low expectations from adults convert into self-defeating attitudes by which students hesitate to ask for help they need. One young man expressed it well: "I don't ask the teacher for nothing. I do it all on my own, or ask my friends for help." "I don't ask the teacher for nothing" is of course a defensive posture, rejecting educators' help before educators refuse his request. These students then convert this defense into an internalized and unrealistic belief in personal responsibility, which colludes with a larger social ideology about "their" fault. In the end, these students do not learn how to ask for or receive help, do not get the help, and, in the likely event of failure, they conclude that it is "my fault." Meritocracy triumphs again.

Perhaps most damaging with respect to future outcomes, some of the youth have elaborated a very punitive ideology that says that mistakes they have made in the past will and should predict negative future outcomes. These youths have committed what psychologists would call a "characterological personal attribution" or "fundamental attribution error" for past mistakes. When people attribute bad outcomes to a moral flaw in themselves, it tends to be difficult to shed the shame, change behavior, and/or believe yourself entitled to future positive outcomes. They have internalized the broader societal message about poor youth: that they *deserve* bad outcomes from the time of their "mistakes" forward (Janoff-Bulman, 2010). Poor children, especially youth of color, tend to be held personally accountable for "mistakes" for which other children are given "second chances," with dire consequences that can last a lifetime (see Ayers, Ayers, Dohrn, & Jackson, 2001).

From Civic Commitments to Structural Alienation

In focus groups and surveys, the California youth express refreshing, deep, strong, and committed civic commitments *toward* family, community, and cultural groups. As Bowen and Bok (1998) demonstrate with youth of color who graduate from college, these are the very young adults most likely to display a commitment to give back to the community, to serve and model an ethic of community spirit. The poor and working-class youth who were interviewed described just such a spirit of citizenship.

While voicing strong local commitments, these young men and women simultaneously reveal a stinging anger at schools that spreads outward toward other governmental institutions and the nation. Their willingness to extend their caring and commitments to the country, to beliefs in democracy, and to a broad moral community called America, has been jeopardized. Frustrated, their alienation stretches from school-ing denied, to governments that betray, to democratic promises that remain unfulfilled.

> It's like what is the Board getting paid for and they can't even come fix our bathroom. They can't even mop our halls. So what they doing with that money?

> They [government] fake like they are [trying to change things]. Because they go to the board meetings and they talk to [Mayor] Willie Brown and everything. And one of my friends is on the committee. And all the [inaudible], Willie Brown says oh, this is what, we're going to do this and everything and he's always talking about how San Francisco is one of the cleanest cities. And he's a wolf ticket seller. I mean, he lies, sorry.

As these comments reveal, the youth want nothing more than what most adults ask for today: *public accountability.* They want someone to assure that the state and the adults will fulfill their legal obligations to educate. They want someone to monitor inequities, intervene, and remedy. The focus group and survey data suggest that students in California's most disadvantaged schools are being educated away from these "obligations of citizenship" and toward civic alienation. They are learning that their needs are irrelevant to policymakers and govern-ment leaders. They speak through a sophisticated discourse of public critique, but don't believe that anyone is listening.

The survey data reveal the suspicions these youths also hold of the economy and the government. As for their future work lives, 42% of the surveyed high school students and 25% of those inter-viewed from middle school believe that labor market prospects will *always* be hard for them and their families. A full 40% of the high school students and half of the middle school students believe that government is designed to serve the "rich." Only one-third of the high school students and 20% of the middle school students think they can make a change in the workings of government. Finally, while 65% of the middle school youth view America as "basical-ly fair and everyone has an equal chance to get ahead," this figure drops to 23% by high school.

These youth reveal a broad-based, sophisticated, and critical con-sciousness of class structures, the stability of inequity, the illusion of mobility, and their "place."

HEARING PROBLEMS: A VIOLATION OF PROCEDURAL JUSTICE

For years, critical scholars of education have heard poor youth and youth of color who attend inadequate public schools tell us about some teachers who don't care, and schools that don't educate, and have observed the resultant anger, shame, stress, and anxiety. These California youth were no exception. As one young man described his concern:

> Because before we had a teacher for like the first three weeks of our multi-culture class and then the teacher didn't have all her credentials so she couldn't continue to teach. And since then we've had like ten different substitutes. And none of them have taught us anything. We just basically do what we wanted in class. We wrote letters, all the class wrote letters to people and they never responded. We still don't have a teacher.

What was striking and distinct about the California focus groups was the powerful voice of institutional betrayal that these youths expressed to audiences who refused to listen. It was not simply the case that these youth, like so many youth across America in under-resourced schools, were denied adequate education and felt helpless. Many of the youth had, in the face of overwhelming odds, tried to secure help. They had spoken up, protested, asked for a "real" teacher or raised an academic concern. What broke their hearts and their spirits was that few adults listened. Even fewer acted.

Students in one high school focus group were most agitated as they contrasted how their schools ignored their requests for quality education, but responded (if superficially) when the state investigated school policies and practices:

> We all walked out, 'cause of the conditions, but they didn't care. They didn't even come out. They sent the police. The police made a line and pushed us back in. Don't you think the principal should have come out to hear what we were upset over? But when the state is coming in, they paint, they fix up the building. They don't care about us, the students, just the state or the city.

These youth describe a doubled experience of disappointment and betrayal. Disappointed by the relative absence of quality faculty and materials, they feel helpless to master rigorous academic material and powerless to solicit effective help. Were that not enough, when these youth do complain, grieve, or challenge the educational inequities they endure, they confront a wall of silence, an institutional "hearing problem." On surveys, only 34% agreed or strongly agreed that "People like me have the ability to change government if we don't like what is happening." As pointed out earlier, these schools are preparing a generation of youth who sustain ethical commitments to family, kin, and community but believe that the government and the nation view them as unworthy and disposable. In such settings, youth report high levels of perceived betrayal by, resistance to, and withdrawal from persons in positions and institutions of public authority (Fabricant & Fine, 2012). These schools are helping to blunt civic engagement and are producing, instead, civic alienation.

COLLEGE GOING, PERHAPS

As the surveys reveal, almost all of these youth expect to graduate from high school and attend college. A full 85% of surveyed high school students consider it likely that they will graduate from their present school, and 91% indicate that they would like to attend college after graduation. However, a full 50% feel that they are "less well" prepared for college than peers throughout the state of California. This represents a serious rise from the 15% of middle school students who report that they feel "less well prepared for college" than peers. The high school students appear to hold high aspirations for college, but are filled with legitimate anxiety about inadequate preparation.

In addition to the high school students who worried about underpreparation, we interviewed a small group of graduates from these schools who are now attending college. Given the high dropout rates of these schools and the small numbers who go on to college, this sample of college-going students represents some of the most academically successful graduates of their schools. Most were surprised to feel less competent than their peers. A number admitted to thoughts of dropping a course or dropping out of college.

> I kept thinking they know more than I do. It seems like I had to do more than them, like I have to go to a lot of tutorial classes. What [my school] has offered me has made my transition to college really difficult. I'm pretty much intimidated in college . . .

I keep thinking, "Am I going to make it?" (Female graduate, now at University of California, Berkeley)

The reflections of these graduates reveal the academic and psychological consequences of academic underpreparation, even for the "stars" of these schools:

High school didn't provide me with any AP or honors classes so I was never exposed to college level work. When I took calculus my first year in college, I couldn't compete. I ended up having to drop the class and take an easier math course. The expectations and standards at [school] were too low. Many students felt like they weren't being exposed to the education they needed. We could see what students at Lowell High were getting, all the AP classes and textbooks. But we had to share most of our books and some we couldn't even take home. (Male graduate, Class of 2000, at UC Berkeley)

These young women and men knew they were top students at their California high schools, and expected to be equally successful in college. Reflecting back on their high school years, these college students all admit that they were underchallenged. While they credit teachers and counselors who "really pushed me . . . taught me to keep an open mind and not to quit," all agree that teachers "could have given more work, they could have been harder on us." When asked, "What did you get from your high schools?" these young women and men report that high school was a context in which they developed a sense of persistence, learning to beat the odds, to struggle, even when no one was in their corner. One young woman, now attending community college, explains, "In high school, I didn't feel any support, especially in terms of college going. I got some basics . . . but I don't feel prepared for college."

CIVICS LESSONS

The schools in question are educating youth toward intellectual mediocrity and alienation, and away from academic mastery and democracy. The youth whom we surveyed and interviewed are the academic "success stories" of impoverished neighborhoods. These are not young women or men who have dropped out. They are the survivors, the believers, whom we are slowly undermining.

Despite the fact that these poor and working-class youth are asking, desperately, for quality educators and challenging curriculum, the evidence suggests that the more years these youth spend in these schools, the more shame, anger, and mistrust they develop, the fewer academic skills they acquire, and the more our diverse democratic fabric frays. While class is traditionally considered a strong predictor of academic success, we have evidence here that academic (ine)quality is an equally strong predictor of class.

Given the political economy of the United States, the racial stratifications, and the broad base of social inequities that confront poor and working-class youth and youth of color, the question for this case asks to what extent do these schools reproduce broad social inequities, worsen them, or reduce their adverse impact (cf., Anyon, 2005)? The evidence presented here suggests that these schools substantially worsen already existent social inequities with psychological, academic, and ultimately economic consequences. One may ask, further, isn't it the case that *all* public schools serving poor and working-class youth, and youth of color, suffer these conditions and produce these outcomes?

There is now well-established evidence of compelling, inquiry-based small schools in Philadelphia, New York City, Chicago, and elsewhere, designed for poor and working-class youth. A number of these schools have fundamentally decoupled the too typical correlation of class and academic success. Built with a commitment to what Lori Chajet (2007) calls *institutional agency*, these schools are designed to resist the "natural" correspondence of class and schooling.

Studies demonstrate that these small public schools can be effectively organized to open opportunities for students, support their strengths and needs, satisfy their yearnings for quality education, prepare them for higher education, and cultivate a strong ethic of community engagement. While the top-down proliferation of small schools in urban districts has become a troubling, quick-fix fad that reflects all the ills of standardization, privatization, gentrification, and high-stakes testing, there is substantial evidence that schools can mediate (not eliminate) the damage of larger social forces. In poor communities, neither academic failure nor alienation is natural or healthy (see Rethinking Schools, 2005).

In contrast to the interviewed students in California, students in these carefully designed schools learn about the possibilities and movements for social change and their responsibilities to participate in creating change (see Anand et al., 2002). Their social critique moves to hope and action, not despair and alienation.

In the California schools in the plaintiff class, students are indeed getting a "civics lesson" in which they are learning to feel powerless, alienated, shameful, angry, and betrayed. The likelihood of democratic engagement by these youths and young adults is fundamentally threatened by their experiences in these schools. Even so, some have tried to speak out about these educational inequities, only to be ignored again. With this lawsuit, they are asking adults to be allies in the struggle for racial and class justice.

The children of California have been twice betrayed: disproportionately, youth of poverty, youth of color, and immigrant youth struggle to persist in some of the worst schools in the nation. And yet their desire to be educated well, with dignity, remains.

Coda: The students and schools were victorious in the *Williams* case; resources and policy transformation moved into these disinvested buildings. And yet at the same time and since, neoliberal moves toward privatization, school closings, high-stakes testing, austerity, corporate charters, and vouchers have occupied, dismantled, and redesigned what constitutes "public education," denying equity and joy to children living in poverty, particularly children of color, immigrants, and students in need of special education. Well into 2017, young people in high school, and on campuses throughout the United States, continue to mobilize for tuition-free public college, community schools, anti-racist school/university designs, inquiry-based assessments, restorative justice, faculty of color, and a moratorium on high-stakes testing, policing, and closing of urban public schools. The struggle for public education is a continuous, fragile braid of racial, labor, and knowledge (in)justice. It defines our history, and our future, and must be fueled by the desires of the young.

CHAPTER 4

"Wicked Problems,"
"Flying Monkeys,"
and Prec(ar)ious Lives
A Matter of Time?

with Andrew Cory Greene and Sonia Sanchez

About 10 years after the *Williams v. California* case described in Chapter 3, I (Michelle) was called back to California for another class action suit, again for students of color, largely immigrant, all poor. This round the lawyers wanted to sue for longer school days, the theory being that poor children suffered far more disruption in their school days than Whiter and wealthier peers. Which was true. And so I and my coauthors were invited to talk, again, to young people and educators about time in school, to listen closely to decide if more hours per day, in deeply under-resourced schools, was really an act of justice. We decided it was not.

In this chapter we rely on the young people as canaries in the neo-liberal mine, for they speak so clearly about *precarity*, the condition of living and being educated in deeply unpredictable times, when public and private institutions are being rapidly destabilized and gentrified, when communities and institutions are traumatized, criminalized, and "redesigned." We offer an interrogation of how intimate and then corporate disruption enters lives and bodies of young people attending high-poverty, segregated schools.

The ironic and tragic ending will be no surprise to the reader: the young people most disrupted today by economic instability, housing and hunger insecurity, gentrification, mass incarceration, and immigration/deportation raids are also attending schools routinely disrupted by school closings, high teacher turnover, over-testing, over-policing, and deep institutional cultures of mistrust. That is, young people who live extremely precarious lives attend profoundly precarious schools, further destabilized by state policy and corporate education reform.

In a nation that has walked away from structural changes and redistribution in wealth, labor, housing, health care, education, and community safety, many battles fought for educational justice take place in courtrooms, like *Brown v. Board of Education* more than 50 years ago. This chapter will take you into one legal case to eavesdrop on how young people embody disruption and mobilize their fortitude for "survivance" (Vizenor, 2008), and how, after spending much time with these young people, we were unconvinced that "more time" in dysfunctional schools would even the playing field.

CURATING TESTIMONY

Educational inequities constitute what Horst Rittel and Melvin Webber (1973) call "wicked problems"—entangled, crusty, reproductive, with many origins and mutations—but courts seek what these same authors call "soluble remedies." The courtroom then becomes an arena for dueling stories. The odds are wildly uneven. The dominant story—for instance, more money doesn't matter or Black students or girls do better "among themselves"—typically enjoys well-funded lawyers, can mobilize lots of evidence, and tucks easily into the Whitestream/elite "common sense" of "lost causes" usually shared by judge and jury, who conclude, "We can't change this." The counternarrative, that money does matter, that racial segregation undermines democracy and education, has to chip away gently at the dominant story with legal logic; empirically demonstrate harm, need, and capacity; and promise that the prescribed remedy will miraculously resolve the scalding, historic, and deep scars of injustice. A heavy lift.

In 2014, we conducted preliminary research for a class action lawsuit contending that poor children deserve more—and enjoy less—"instructional time" because of violence in and out of school, lockdowns, police–student incidents, 40% long-term substitute teachers, immigration raids, bad water, chipping paint, unsafe conditions, overreliance on testing, etc. A team of civil rights lawyers from California invited us to gather quantitative and qualitative data about disparities in instructional time that affect students in schools of high concentration of poverty. They had already amassed testimony from young people about the various routine intrusions in the day and wanted a more systematic analysis from young people in middle and high school, and their educators, about the kinds of events, dynamics, surprising and spontaneous activities that occur in low-income schools and that interrupt teaching and learning. At the time, John Rogers and Nicole Mirra (2014) had just begun a comprehensive analysis of disparities in instructional time in schools throughout California and have since concluded that students who attend extremely poor high schools lose, on average, 25 days a year—almost 14% of the year—to in-school disruptions, including subs, lockdowns, drills, and immigration and police raids.

We were hired to gather various kinds of materials—narratives, surveys, maps, performances—from students and educators in high-poverty schools about "loss of" or "need for" "extra" learning time. We conducted a quantitative and qualitative assessment of systematic disruptions of instructional time, as experienced by students and teachers. A total of 49 students and 17 faculty, from Los Angeles, Oakland, and San Francisco, participated in the research. The legal team pre-arranged four focus groups of students and three groups of teachers. All focus groups lasted approximately 120 minutes, and at the end of each group students and educators were provided with a $75 gift card for participation in the study.

The sample included students who were all attending high schools of significant poverty, with the exception of two middle school students in transition from the 8th to 9th grade and three recently graduated high school students. Two of the student groups were held in summer programs on race/culture and education at major universities. One student identified as White, one Asian American/Pacific Islander, one "other," nine biracial, 15 African American, and 21 Latina/o/Chicana/o. Parental and students' consents were obtained for all focus group participants.

We facilitated the focus groups of teens and educators with a common protocol. First they completed a short quantitative survey about school/work life, checking off "all that apply" from a list of "intrusions on time" and "frequency of occurrence" compiled from the depositions and from the existent literature. After completing the surveys, each participant was given blank paper and magic markers and asked to draw a map of "how time feels in your body in school." The cognitive/identity mapping prompt has been developed by Valerie Futch and Michelle Fine (2014), extending the work of Milgram and Jodelet (1976) and Winnicott (1971) before them. Identity maps are gathered to elicit creative, representational landscapes of experience and affect. After a discussion of the maps and the "intrusions," for the final 30 minutes we asked the students and educators to describe or enact ped-agogical moments "when time flies; when you feel like you are really learning and not even paying attention to the clock." This exercise drew from the work of Augusto Boal's *Theatre of the Oppressed* (1979).

The map prompt was simple: "What does time feel like in your body in school?" In the nearly 50 maps we collected, students wrote poetry and drew wildly divergent images of hands flying high in ad-vanced classes separated by perforated lines from heads on desks be-hind prison bars in remedial classes. Other young people sketched snails, clocks whose hands have stopped, long-term substitute teach-ers showing the films *Nemo* and *Juice* to high school students in disin-vested schools, question marks, talking with friends, heads on desks, enthusiasm, and alienation.

"Flying Monkeys"

In our first focus group, Carlos drew a picture of himself and his class-mates walking along "the yellow brick road; we take tests, some of us do well and keep going, we have no idea where, and some fall off the road. I have no idea if there is anyone really behind the green curtains. But there are these flying monkeys that keep getting in the way" (see Figure 4.1).

Crises at Home. The other students followed up: "Yeah, I get what you mean about flying monkeys." Caro interjected, "My brothers are both in prison but they call me every morning to make sure I am ready to go to school, they worry about me so much." Jeanne chimed in: "Not to be, like you know, pity or anything, I just lost my little brother this summer, so um, and that was something that was really hard for my family to deal with. He was loved by a lot of people. He was only like twelve, and um . . . it, it, it all has to do with what you're anchored in."

A few moments later, Marcello interjected, "My dad was deported last year and my life has been pretty rough since then." The theme of "flying monkeys" became a telling metaphor for the structures, policies, traumas, and the systematic unpredictability from which their young lives dangled. A vivid metaphor for precarity. Most of the young people we spoke with were experiencing substantial difficulties at home, on the streets, in their families. A full 50% of the youth we surveyed indicated that from once a month to once a year they did not attend school because they had to take care of family responsibilities;

**Figure 4.1.
Behind the
Green Curtain**

another 8% answered the same question, "once a week, once a day or all the time."

Students wrote on surveys or told us in focus groups: "My mother has severe mental illness, and I try to help her," or "My father has cancer, and I hang out with him." Likewise, in focus groups students described siblings in prison, troubles at home, being adopted or in foster care, involvement with the juvenile justice system, participation in gangs. Even students who were flourishing academically mentioned substantial life difficulties and yearned for support, such as Caro, introduced earlier:

> But like she said, we have a lot of problems like people who go to jail. Just like to be open, all my brothers are right now. . . . And they all, they're still calling me every day, like, "What are you doing?" I told them I was going to a meeting [the focus group of the current study] and they said, "No way, you don't have transportation." And I was like, "You guys, I need to be able to take the bus," and it's like, "Yeah I'm going to go to school, and it's like I need to focus here."

**Figure 4.2.
A Question
of Time**

Asked to explain his map of a clock surrounded by question marks (see Figure 4.2), Edward told us: "But it's just a clock with a bunch of question marks, because how I think of time is, it's you never really know what to expect from it, . . . I don't know, I think you can never trust, you know. It's always unexpected."

It was as if Edward were the consulting artist for critical theorist Isabelle Lorey (2015), "Precarization means living with the unforeseeable, with contingency . . . The conceptual composition of 'precarious' can be described in the broadest sense as insecurity and vulnerability, destabilization and endangerment" (p. 10).

School Disruptions and Surveillance. Hyperaware of the fluidity, predictability, and velocity of precarity, the students leapt from discussing crises at home and in their communities to enumerating the constant changes in school structure. For example, Whitney said:

> Um, I was thinking that um, like, our school, alone R.H.S. has had ten changes in schedule and um yeah, and like um, we used to be a big school and then we had tracks, and then it went from tracks to learning academies, and then to small schools. So we have a lot of changes, we've been having changes for the past nine years, so um I think something that keeps us grounded is like—at least for me—family, but at school everything is like really unstable, at least for us. Not our teachers and stuff, because I do love my teachers but I see how they're stressing out about how they're going to be able to help us. Like how can they help

us when they don't have a school to back them up. Like they're not sure if they're going to have their jobs the upcoming year . . .

Youth intuit how lack of stability in school design can affect students' grades, interrupt mentoring relationships, and may depress aspirations or facilitate pushout. Raymond said:

> Um, she [the principal] kept mentioning the changes in school, and um, I was—she said that um, there's changes and stuff, and if it works good then not, you know, they change it again. And if it works, like she said, it's good, but if it doesn't work we're the ones going through the changes, so we're the ones being affected.

Knowing all too well, in their bodies, the findings that Rogers and Mirra (2014) would report months later, on inequitable instructional time, these students narrated disruptions and inequities, teacher absences, emergency lockdowns, and excessive preparation for standardized tests. They elaborate the affective and social psychological tremors that follow when chaos reigns.

Perhaps it is no surprise that in racially segregated schools of high poverty, institutional instability, high teacher turnover, substantial use of long-term subs, and heavy investment in police and school safety officers, *banal chaos* permeates the air. While eager to lavish praise on "teachers who care," for the most part these young people characterized their schools as untrustworthy and experienced some educators as disrespectful. They noticed, astutely, the differential treatment of students in AP and those in the "regular" classes, as noted in Figure 4.3. As if they were referencing the literature on the school-to-prison pipeline, students describe educational triage where top students are cultivated with opportunities for dignity, inquiry, and creativity and struggling students are more often contained and managed by a punitive culture.

> *Meg:* Big, ginormous rifles, like, on their back, just walking, "Hey, good morning." It's normal at our school.
> *Researcher:* What rifles?
> *Meg:* Like, there's a police station—yes, rifles.
> *Jalill:* Oh, I was just going to add onto the thing like talking about how our schools resemble jails . . . recently our principal that I guess came to the school just like two years ago or something

Figure 4.3. Effects of Tracking

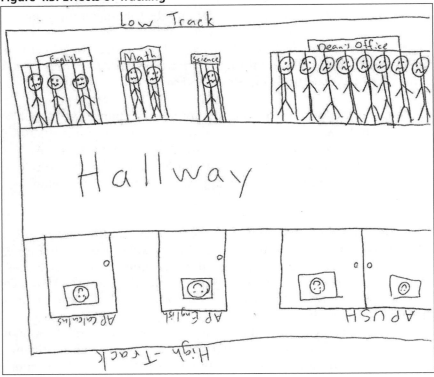

> like that, he just um brought in this new policy where they do random searches with like dogs.
>
> *Chris:* It's not even random. They pick like the lower classes, and then—I swear—and they're like, everyone count off numbers, one, two, three, they keep track, who picked number three? And they're like, all the three's step outside. And the dog will search you. And it's never an AP class or anything like that. It's always the lower—
>
> *Jalill:* Our school, they randomly search your locker and then leave a note in there that just says, "We searched your locker."

Teacher Turnover and Long-Term Substitutes. Young people (and their educators) described the human toll of school-level disruption, surveillance, and policing worsened by, predictive of, and resulting from high rates of teacher absenteeism, turnover, and use of long-term subs. Some of these schools have, at varied points in the academic year, as much as 40% teacher turnover, with an associated infusion of long-term subs (see Fine, Burns, Payne, & Torre, 2004). After many of our informants complained about long-term subs, I asked, "So what's wrong with long-term subs?"

> *Misha:* In the ninth grade, I had this Spanish teacher, he was like the best Spanish teacher, I was going to do advanced Spanish, but he got fired towards the end. Um, so this substitute came in . . . so we got this substitute . . . He doesn't know Spanish. He's asking the students how to pronounce words. How are you a Spanish teacher and not know Spanish? So it was like—he messed up my whole Spanish experience. . . . Subs are just awful.
>
> *Ivory:* They reject everything you tell them, but they're not present during your like, your daily routine. And I feel like when they're there for a long time, and you fall out of your routine, you fall out of your learning habits. They have like excess power issues going on in their lives.
>
> *Darren:* Yes! They do!
>
> *Mocha:* "I'm in control, I don't care what you say, you talk, I will—I don't care if you're like, you could be crying, I don't care, get out of my classroom, (?)" like they're just so. . . .
>
> *Spring:* I hate the subs that come in, try to take charge, standing over you the whole period—that just makes you want to be defiant, in my opinion. I hate that.
>
> *Darren:* The good subs, they'll come in, like she said, they'll have an assignment, and like, "All right, I need y'all to just keep it down a little, don't get too loud, you can talk, do your assignment" . . . And we'd be like, "All right, we're good!"

And one young woman admitted:

> I really liked my teacher who I didn't know was a long-term sub, and then one day she said, "Tomorrow your real teacher will be coming." I felt so bad, I didn't even know she was a sub, why didn't she tell us? Couldn't she trust us?

Students told stories about feeling hurt and betrayed when they started to develop relationships with "teachers," in some cases only to find out the day before the teacher departed that their "teacher" was a long-term substitute.

Psychiatrist Mindi Fullilove (2009) theorizes the embodied sense of uncontrollable and persistent change she calls "root shock." Fullilove studies extensively the cumulative social and psychic consequences of uprooting, disruptions of relationships, and erosion of communities of meaning, particularly within communities of color. She argues that people who have been displaced and surrounded by constant change experience traumatic stress reactions to the loss of some or all of their emotional ecosystems. These psychological concerns transpire not only because communities are changing, but, more important, because *residents feel they have no control over the vast changes in their lives*, changes that threaten the intimate webs of social relationships that help them endure hard times. Unfortunately the institutional conditions that predominate in high-poverty schools are precisely the conditions that threaten the thin, fragile bonds that might protect children and might support their educators.

Lack of Authentic Learning. Even when the teachers are "real" and "certified," students explained that most of the day is consumed not with authentic learning, inquiry, or creativity but with preparation for standardized tests. Students experience the intense focus on testing as a betrayal of teaching as a relationship built on rich, inquiry-based, culturally rich practices. When educators feel pressured to "deliver" content that students are supposed to "learn" and reproduce as a correct answer, the elegant choreography of pedagogy is disrupted; the give and take is shattered; the synchronicity and serendipity of learning flattens:

> *Researcher:* How much of your day is spent on test-prep?
> *Raiza:* I feel like the whole year, we're preparing for tests.
> *Others students:* Yeah. Yeah, the whole year.
> *Researcher:* Well, do you mean actually by yourself, studying for a test?
> *Carlos:* I feel like it's used as an excuse sometimes.
> *Researcher:* Ooh, say why.
> *Carlos:* Like, we're in class, and then like you question, "why are we doing all this? "Oh, the test." "Oh, this test." "Oh, you have to study for this." And then it's like, what, and then you get to the test, and then you just get it over with, and then you're like, you're done, but you move onto the next one.
> *Lunnette:* I feel like my teachers are kind of different. Like my AP . . . U.S. history teacher, Ms (X), she's like, "I hate that I have

to prep you for this test because I want to be able to break this content down and really get into it," like we'd have Socratic seminars and everything she's like, "I wish we could spend more time on one thing," she's like, "But I'm on schedule and my first like priority" even if it's not her own, "is to make sure that you score well on this test," like that's what the class is for, right, an AP class, so you can take um, an AP test and get college credit, but she's like, "If we had more time, like I would dedicate more time to make sure that you guys are learning everything not that—" because we have to rush, it's a lot of content that we have to fit into the time you start until like the AP test, so yeah.

Young people who are most vulnerable to the physical and emotional dislocations of family, home, school, language, nation, and relationships are also hypervulnerable to neoliberal educational reforms. That is, low-income, predominantly Black schools are targeted for closure, while nearby charters selectively enroll and then expel students from these buildings. In highly segregated low-income public schools, teachers are frequently removed, transfer, or exit mid-year. Long-term subs are commonplace, teachers are evaluated based on student test scores, and deep inquiry work and creativity have been sacrificed for memorization. Despite all that has been written on the fundamental importance of *trust, stability, continuity, and sustainability of relationships in school,* particularly for the most marginalized Black and Latino students, urban educational reform has been characterized by staccato-like disruptions for the poor and smooth continuities for the rich. It was astonishing to listen as these young people narrated with eloquence the predictability of the unpredictable. And yet they know, as if in muscle memory, what real learning feels like.

Exceptional Moments—Experiencing Flow

We spent the final 30 minutes of our focus groups asking the youth (and the educators) to describe times when they felt that time in school "flew," when they were "so engaged you forgot to look at the clock." In some groups people answered individually. In others they worked in small groups and performed scenes of experiences when instructional time "flies." Across focus groups, students described spaces in which "the traffic light is on green" (see Figure 4.4), it feels like things "just flow," "teachers stand in the back of the classroom as

**Figure 4.4.
Time Goes Fast,
Slow, or Regular**

*sometimes it goes fast, slow, or regular.
It changes.*

**Figure 4.5.
Time at a
Snail's Pace**

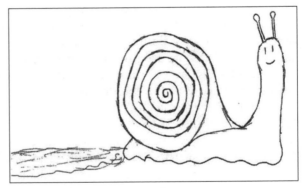

students direct their learning" or times when "students are enjoying what they're doing so much we all forget it's lunch time."

Existential philosopher Maxine Greene (1977) has written thoughtfully about the distinction between *anesthetic experiences*—which are deadening, numbing, and put us to sleep—and *aesthetic experiences*—which are provocative and awakening. In our focus groups, we heard about many experiences, both anesthetic and aesthetic. In one group of youth, the maps were shockingly consistent sketches of heads on desks, sleeping, teachers showing movies, one perfectly still snail (see Figure 4.5). State-sponsored anesthesia. And yet, in the final 30 minutes, when asked to describe situations when class time flew, when meaningful teaching and learning filled the air, students and educators alike offered up stories that resonate with what psychologist Mikel Csikszentmihalyi calls "flow." "Flow" involves the "subjective phenomenology of intrinsically motivated activity." "Viewed through the experiential lens of flow," Csikszentmihalyi and his coauthor Nakamura have argued, "a good life is one that is characterized by complete absorption in what one does" and involves

> intense and focused concentration on what one is doing in the present moment, merging of action and awareness, loss of reflective self-consciousness, a sense that one can control one's actions, a sense that time has passed faster than normal; experience of the activity as intrinsically rewarding. . . . (Nakamura & Csikszentmihalyi, 2002, pp. 89–90)

Just as a culture of trust requires a community of dignity and support for educators, so too "flow" for students is not simply internal to an individual but requires a "dynamic system of person and environment" among adolescents and adults (Nakamura & Csikszentmihalyi, 2002, p. 99). Fortunately we had the opportunity to hear about and witness rich engagements in a number of multicultural, activist learning spaces, including a group of students from the Bay Area who, at the time, were attending a summer program on Ethnic Studies at a local university. In a community center in Oakland, Marisol broke the ice to speak about moments of meaningful learning, and these moments pivoted on developing critical literacies to read the world, as if she were channeling my old friend Paulo Freire (1970):

> Well, in some classes it feels like they're never going to end . . . [but] for like a class that I really enjoy was, um . . . my ethnic studies class. Yeah, it was interesting. . . . We got to learn about other people's like ethnicities, and like the history of like people of color and why—what they went through, and like, the things that . . . like, we got [to] learn the counternarrative about how they like actually did good things, and sometimes like how white—like, how people . . . how white people like took like credit for people of color's ideas and stuff. So I actually got to learn all about like that. . . . My teacher recommended this book, *The New Jim Crow*, so I tried to get it. So yeah, I'm going to read it.

At the summer youth-organizing project on the campus of UC Berkeley, when asked about their regular schools, the students narrated and drew the kinds of schools we had been hearing about: few windows, low expectations, and a grueling history of rotating long-term subs. However, prior to the group interview, we had unwittingly walked through one of their Youth Leadership sessions at the MultiCultural Community Center. Standing beneath a colorful mural of Cesar Chavez, Huey Newton, and varied youth of color, the young people were in deep discussion, debate, and full-bodied engagement. We asked them to explain the difference; what kinds of learning are engaging, empowering? The arms began to wave:

"Learning about my history," or "excuse me, but what we are learning is Caucasian history." Most of these students attend relatively traditional schools; they nevertheless came alive in their discussions of summer engagement with critical literacies, referencing Ethnic Studies, Youth Leadership, and Critical Pedagogy classes at UCLA and UC Berkeley. The young people were contesting what Damien Sojoyner (2016), in his text, *First Strike: Educational Enclosures in Black Los Angeles,* describes as technologies of control and enclosure that dominate contemporary public school classrooms in communities of color: the heightened securitization of public schools, the erasure of ethnic studies/whitening of the curriculum, and the hyperdominance of testing and sorting. The students thirst for cultural history, and for analyses of injustice and the struggle to be recognized and educated. Their appetites were whetted by simple openings of summer engagements with critical pedagogy and organizing.

> All right. So since I'm a public speaker, I'm good at—or I often write speeches, so [I will] start off with a quote from Martin Luther King Jr.: "We shouldn't repent for the acts of bad people, but instead for the silence of those who are good." I feel the time I waste submitting to the educational system could instead be used to learn. To learn my culture, properly. To learn how to empower my people and myself. Time to learn how to create change. But unfortunately, I must get back to my homework.

As Carter describes above, young people seek an education that helps them analyze critically their current circumstances, values their critique and feeds their desire, introduces them to histories of struggle and possibility, and equips them with skills to build a different tomorrow, even in the swamp of structural, existential, and embodied precarity.

At the multicultural leadership project, we asked about "teachers who made a difference." Monique piped up, "There was a teacher who said you are gonna be a great reader, I am going to help you—and she handed me a book that I couldn't read and she said: 'we are going to do this together'." Vicente added, "I just love teachers who put red marks all over my paper but then show me how to write better."

Students who were engaged in workshops on multicultural leadership, Youth Particularly Action Research (YPAR) projects, and youth activism seminars at Berkeley and UCLA spoke with a vibrancy about learning "our history—with all due respect, we are tired of learning Caucasian history"; producing critical knowledge, pursuing research, writing poetry, leading campaigns. The distinction between their in-school experiences and their experiences in these critical youth organizing/leadership contexts was striking.

Educational Context Matters

Listening closely, we learned three things:

1. Beware the seductive appeal of *technical solutions to wicked problems* in policy or in court. While many programs instituted as "longer school day" are rich, critical, inquiry-based, and grounded in youth leadership, simply mandating more time in toxic settings is not a civil rights agenda.
2. It is a cruel policy irony, another installment of racialized state violence, that the *young people with the most personal, material, and existential precarity attend schools that are most vulnerable to policy-based disruption*, implemented often in the name of "protection" or "support."
3. Even in circumstances of massive disinvestment and civic betrayal, *young people in highly precarious circumstances nevertheless yearn for opportunities* to be respected, recognized, and educated; to dive into critical histories; to create opportunities for and with their communities; and to mobilize for educational justice. Despairing about their schools, these young people nevertheless have a thirst to be educated.

By listening to the voices of young people speaking across very different educational settings, we learned just how much context matters. Demographically identical youth were so passionately engaged in settings that invited inquiry, critical history, creativity, and deep participation, and so fundamentally alienated in settings corroded by neoliberal reforms. More instructional time is of course a human right, particularly for young people routinely denied equal time in school.

And yet more time in systematically disinvested and dehumanizing buildings is no one's idea of justice.

In our last focus group, in a community setting where there was more despair than oxygen, after we explained the purpose of the focus groups and that the lawsuit framed more instructional time as a civil right long denied, one young man said, "Lady, you seem really nice. Please don't make us go to school for longer days. It already feels like a jail."

Ultimately we chose not to testify. We met with the lawyers and explained that we could not testify for the civil right to more instructional time in schools that violate the dignity of the young. We continue to work with lawyers, youth, and community activists, advocating for more time in worthy educational settings. These narratives obligated us to trace back the literatures on precarity, and to unearth how contemporary educational "reforms" and state policies exacerbate the disruptions that already disassemble young lives of color growing up in poverty.

THE CUMULATIVE WEIGHT OF GROWING UP IN PRECARITY

Whether explicitly stated or not, every political effort to manage populations involves a tactical distribution of precarity . . . regarding whose life is grievable and worth protecting, and whose life is ungrievable or marginally or episodically grievable.

—Puar, 2012, p. 170

Jasbir Puar asks, "Whose life is worth protecting?" as Lauren Berlant (2007) writes that precarity is the "fuse to slow death." Drawing on the narratives of young people in California, we learn that precarity is multi-scalar. Structurally, precarity derives from a racialized political economy that has systemically disinvested in opportunities for low-income youth of color, degrading material conditions, disrupting the living/learning, severing intimate relations in their schools, and unleashing the unnerving predictability of impending disaster. While we may all experience an existential sense of precarity in an increasingly violent world, the structural consequences of precarity are deeply regionalized in the Global South, raced and classed. Within the United States, the pooling and coagulation of precarity-inducing policies can be found most viscerally and viciously in the swollen ankles of communities of color, poverty, and immigration.

Statistical Landscape

A quick journey through the now familiar statistical landscape reveals the entwined circuits of dispossession in Black and Latino communities, and the intensification of dispossession and segregation in the last decade by neoliberal corporate educator reforms racing through urban America, dismantling and disrupting.

In ways deeply racialized and classed, public institutions, communities, educators, and youth attached to "high poverty" segregated schools are most vulnerable to fluctuations in the federal and state budget, neoliberal policy regimes, the flipping of real estate, aggressive policing, incarceration and immigrant sweeps, and school closings. These conditions are forms of what Rosa Luxembourg (1913/2003) and later David Harvey (2003) would call *accumulation by dispossession* and have worsened significantly in the past decade.

In 2000, one in eight public schools was classified by the U.S. Department of Education as "high poverty"; by 2011 that figure leaped to one out of five public schools, in which 75% or more of students qualify for free or reduced-price lunch. The National Center for Children in Poverty (nccp.org) reports that in 2013, 44% of children lived in low-income families (poor and near poor), a figure that increased from 39% in 2007. The National Center on Family Homelessness (familyhomeless ness.org) reports that one in every 30 children in the United States is homeless. The 2011–2012 figures swelled by 10% in one year, estimated to be 72% higher than before the recession. By 2015, the center reports dramatic increases, among homeless children, in the numbers of children with disabilities, children who are limited in their English proficiency, and children who arrived in the United States as unaccompanied minors (United States Interagency Council on Homelessness, 2015).

Family insecurity has been dramatically magnified and racialized in recent history as a consequence of U.S. policies and practices around immigration, criminalization, and housing. For the year 2011–2012, Human Rights Watch reports that the nearly 400,000 persons deported that year left behind more than 202,000 American children (hrw. org/news/2015/01/08/border-enforcement-policies-ensnare-parents-us-citizen-children). More than 2.7 million children in the United States have an incarcerated parent, and approximately 10 million have experienced parental incarceration at some point in their lives. These include 1 in 9 African American children (11.4%), 1 in 26 Latino children (3.5%), and 1 in 57 White children (1.8%) (Correctional Association of New York, 2007).

The Devastation of School Closings

School closings have emerged as a singular, routinized, and devastating educational policy ripping through communities of color. The National Center for Educational Statistics of the U.S. Department of Education (2016) reports that in the 2000–2001 school year, 717 traditional public schools were closed. In 2010–2011, 1,069 schools were closed, largely in (gentrifying) cities and primarily in African American communities (U.S. Department of Education, 2016). From 2000 to 2012 a total of 20,709 schools were closed. In *Death by a Thousand Cuts: Racism, School Closures and Public School Sabotage*, the writers from the Journey for Justice Alliance (2013) offer a detailed analysis of the consequences of school closing as an education-reform strategy, documenting cuts that disproportionately affected students and teachers in Black and Latino urban communities. A cross-city analysis of "the color of school closures" in Chicago, New York, and Philadelphia reveals that schools slated for closing were 88% Black and 94% low-income in Chicago, 81% Black and 93% low-income in Philadelphia, and 59% Black and 82% low-income in New York City (see Galletta, 2012; Schott Foundation, 2013).

Studies have tracked students displaced by school closings in Cleveland, Chicago, and Denver and consistently find that displaced students lose relationships and trust and suffer academically. In Cleveland, Galletta (2012) finds that most displaced students have already attended five, six, and sometimes as many as seven elementary schools, and in Chicago, De la Torre and Gwynne (2009) find that 94% of the displaced students evidenced no gains beyond their expected development.

Children and youth living in poverty and attending schools of concentrated poverty are both more likely to need, and less likely to have, access to schools of stability, relational trust, and consistent instruction of high quality. These young people are also more likely to experience high rates of school transitions, disruptions, and school closures. As Eccles and Roeser (2011) argue:

> [these transitions] are particularly troublesome in our highly mobile society to which teachers represent one of the last stable sources of nonparental role models for adolescents. (p. 229).

The aggressive school closure movement in largely Black and Latino and immigrant communities further destabilizes youth growing up in over-policed and under-educated low-income communities in urban America, accelerating the velocity and penetration of gentrification and precarity, and undermining relationships between schools and communities, families and educators, and youth and local public institutions.

At this moment in history, public educational policy is deeply influenced by corporate reform strategies, as illustrated in Christensen's (2015) model of Disruptive Innovation—testing, followed by school closings and charter school expansion, disrupting tenuous relations in low-income communities of color. Disrupting the old to create space to build the new results in severing ties to history and community and between individuals, while softening spaces for new market-based reforms. Communities of color have long been colonized, disrupted, and readied for profit-making. These communities, like all communities natural and human made, are ecosystems, and disruption ripples out, with vast, multisector adverse consequences. These adverse consequences of dispossession in low-income communities, as Fine and Ruglis (2009) have argued, spill across sectors and generations, dismantling, disrupting, and destabilizing. And then a low-cost "option" is offered, a corporate charter or voucher, peeling some away from the community, seduced in desperation to consider options to chronic miseducation.

BUILDING SCHOOLS FOR RACIAL, EDUCATIONAL, AND LABOR JUSTICE

Adolescents of color, in poverty and/or living in immigrant households, have more adverse events in their own lives than privileged peers; their troubles are more likely to affect other domains of life; their schools are less likely to be "safe havens" that might buffer trauma. We now know that the associated stresses of disruption and erratic stressors move under the skin, into the bloodstream, throughout the body.

Neuroscientist Bruce McEwen (2000, 2012) has studied the cumulative impact of social stressors on young bodies; he coined the term *allostatic load* to represent the cumulative wear and tear on the body's systems due to repeated adaptation to stressors, affecting blood pressure, cholesterol levels, and hemoglobin levels. This body of research is summarized simply by Velasquez-Manoff (2013): "the higher you are in the social hierarchy, the better your health, because . . . the stress that kills . . . is characterized by a lack of a sense of control over one's fate." These epidemiologists have discovered that the only effective mediator of children's well-being, despite the onslaught of trauma and stress, are strong, grounded relationships with family, educators, or youth organizations. Bryk and Schneider (2003) have documented the powerful impact of a culture of "relational trust" on individual and collective academic gains. Likewise, educational theorist and researcher Linda Powell Pruitt (2000/2011) thoughtfully conceptualized how under-resourced schools, serving low-income children, with committed but burdened faculties, can nevertheless create *holding environments*, for educators and youth:

> Teachers are being asked to take on new tasks with little support and shifting goals, under considerable scrutiny about outcomes . . . workers in organizations dealing with these kinds of challenges need more than what has traditionally been studied as social support on the job . . . human beings must be "held" to develop well. These "holding environments" are "temporary bases to which people retreat for respite, support, help" . . . enabling them to recover their bearings and figure out what to do. (p. 42)

McEwen (2012), Pruitt (2000/2011), Bryk and Schneider (2003), and Fullilove (2009)—a neuroscientist, clinical psychologist, educational policy analysts, and psychiatrist—concur that relationships matter; stability matters; dignity matters. While schools cannot clean up the residue of inequality gaps, state violence, relentless racism, and xenophobia, they can be designed to respect children, their families, and educators; preserve relationships; cultivate inquiry; and invite creativity. At present, however, schools in low-income communities of color are themselves being disrupted and dismantled by the same corporate forces that have undermined the economy, housing stock, middle-class wages, democratic participation in local governance, and the fragile threads of our social fabric; these schools have been infiltrated by testing manufacturers, policing, and technologies of control.

At present, more poor children of color are significantly dispossessed and living precarious lives than was true a decade ago. For schools to be effective, equitable, and accountable to children and families, high-poverty schools require stability, support, professional development, and practices that build trust among educators, between community and school, and among the youth and the staff.

And schools serving low-income Black and Latino students—both immigrant and U.S.-born—not only inherit bodies that tremble from substantial structural precarity; these schools themselves enforce policies that induce disruption and punishment.

But these are human-made decisions that can be unmade. Despite years—and generations—of institutional betrayal, young people growing up in poverty yearn for educational spaces that are filled with respect for their biographies and capacities and for who they are, and who they might become. They hunger for educators who might help them read for pleasure and research idiosyncratic questions. They are eager to enter into rich, complex dialogue about matters of social import with educators and peers. They crave spaces where they belong, are treated with dignity, and can produce work of meaning. They are asking us for no more than what is their human right: a dignified and sustained education filled with challenge and support, possibility and stretch. These young people deserve public policies that honor continuity, community, democracy, relationships, inquiry, and creativity—all that elites take for granted in their children's private or public schools.

Contemporary neoliberal reforms sever schools from communities; seduce motivated students out of their neighborhoods to exit for (often empty) promises of mobility; close neighborhood schools and reopen them for Other people's children; banish multicultural and antiracist curricula and replace them with standardized bits of decontextualized worksheets and tests. These reforms viscously exacerbate the precarity infesting low-income communities of color; they constitute a material and psychological virus undermining the core of our collective humanity.

But alternative campaigns and movements are sprouting across the nation:

- The movement for finance equity and community schools, advocated by Journeys for Justice, activist groups in New York City, Newark, Detroit, and Chicago
- "Grow your own teachers," in which performance assessment and restorative justice take seriously the precarious conditions in which low-income students survive, and the need for schools to be grounded in, governed by, and accountable to communities as pods of democracy, community engagement, antiracist organizing, intellectually thrilling and culturally engaged curriculum, and the arts

- Community schools for justice in which health services, social workers, community organizers, educators, lawyers, and youth come together to resist the extraction industries of Disruptive Innovation, and to honor, recognize, and engage the tragic and vibrant brilliance of those born in precarity.

CHAPTER 5

Just Methods
Historic and Contemporary Laboratories of Democratic Knowledge Production

Sometime between 1929 and 1935, from a prison cell in fascist Italy, Antonio Gramsci wrote: "The crisis consists precisely in the fact that the old is dying and the new cannot be born; in this interregnum a great variety of morbid symptoms appear" (1971, p. 276). Almost a century later, we are saturated in morbid symptoms in the "interregnum." In this chapter I review a set of critical community research projects hatched in social movements within the United States (late 1800s–present). Each project sought to interrupt "crisis," reveal "morbid symptoms," and mobilize movements for liberation and solidarity— with the humble tools of critical science. All were founded in grassroots movements for social justice; most emerged in neighborhoods under siege (from coal mining companies, from conditions of imposed structural poverty, and from within prisons, for example), and all involved complex and wildly diverse research teams stitching together researchers from universities or progressive research centers with community members intimately affected by inequity. The projects sought to document structural violence and also to generate radical alternatives. While this review focuses on the history of critical community PAR in the United States, I recommend reading about diverse indigenous Maori projects in New Zealand in Linda Tuhiwai Smith's 1999 volume *Decolonizing Methodologies*, and for a rich set of projects crafted in the Global South see Boaventura de Sousa Santos's volume *Epistemologies of the South: Justice Against Epistemicide* (2014). I encourage you to order a copy of *The People's Knowledge and Participatory Action Research: Beyond the White Walled Labyrinth of the Academy* (People's Knowledge Editorial Collective, 2016), download the documents pulled together in the original *We Charge Genocide* (1951) letter to the U.N. General Assembly, and then the International Katrina Rita Tribunal (see King, 2015), review *The Apartheid Archives* compiled by Garth Stevens, Norman Duncan, and

Derek Hook (2013), check out *Memoscopio Project: Testimonios from the World March for Peace and Nonviolence* (Muñoz-Proto, Lyon, Castillo, & Battistella, 2013; memoscopio.org); and I ask readers to excavate local instances of buried collective work born in "freedom dreams" (Kelley, 2003). The passionate fossils of these projects can be found everywhere, if we dare to look.

Before going further, I want to add a note about my choice of terminology in the title of this chapter. My use of "laboratories" derives from "laboratory studies" in the tradition of Karin Knorr Cetina (1999), Bruno Latour and Steve Woolgar (1979), Jill Morawski (1997), and Emily Martin (2016) as spaces for the production of and reflection on critical scientific inquiry. Further I recognize the term *democratic* to be highly contested, but it sits, for the moment, as a strategic placeholder where others may have inserted *critical, public, indigenous, participatory, insurgent*, or even *borderlands* research. And of course one needs to explain "science." I draw from a long legacy of critical researchers working with and alongside social movements, including Orlando Fals-Borda (1985), Paulo Freire (1970), Appalachian scholar and activist John Gaventa (1980), Indigenous Maori scholar Linda Tuhiwai Smith (1999), El Salvadorian liberation psychologist Ignacio Martín-Baró (1990), and Brazilian sociologist Boaventura de Sousa Santos (2014). All argue for community-based, participatory research by, with, and alongside communities, engaged to contest the hegemonic academic hold on what is read as valid science and to widen the construct of "expertise."

HISTORIC VEINS OF PARTICIPATORY RESEARCH

In an essay published posthumously in *Commonweal* magazine, "Reparations: Attention Must be Paid," Ignacio Martín-Baró, one of the Jesuit priests murdered in El Salvador in 1989, a faculty member at the Universidad Centroamericana and liberation psychologist, wrote on the urgency and the humbling limits of documenting State violence on the people:

> It is clear that no one is going to return to the imprisoned dissident his youth; to the young woman who has been raped her innocence; to the person who has been tortured his or her integrity. Nobody is going to return the dead and the disappeared to their families. What can and must be publicly restored [are] the victims' names and their dignity, through a

formal recognition of the injustice of what has occurred, and, wherever possible, material reparation. . . . Those who clamour for social reparation are not asking for vengeance. Nor are they blindly adding difficulties to a historical process that is already by no means easy. On the contrary, they are promoting the personal and social viability of a new society, truly democratic. (1990, p. 184)

With passion and anguish, Martín-Baró narrates why bearing witness matters—how necessary it is to excavate evidence of State-born atrocities, document the consequences, and hold the State accountable if a society is to move forward. Martín-Baró embodies a (recessive) strain of courageous social science, fueled by commitments to justice and reparations, dedicated to serious and systematic inquiry, and impelled by what Robin Kelley (2003) would call freedom dreams. While we must acknowledge the long and more dominant colonial history of academic social sciences misrepresenting and exploiting marginalized communities of color and poverty, and engaging in research as an extraction industry, in this chapter, in an effort to add to the project of decolonizing social inquiry, I seek to tell another story about critical science and democracy. I want to make legible the relatively eclipsed history of critically engaged research, undertaken by racially and economically diverse collectives of researchers, activists, community members, educators, students, and sometimes musicians/artists, alongside communities in crisis, to advance social justice. We will unearth and investigate how "fugitive spaces" (Harney & Moten, 2013) of democratic production of knowledge have been and can be cultivated as a resource for building more just communities, reframing participatory policies, and stitching fragile solidarities.

Since the late 1800s (and probably before), delicately designed social research projects have been rooted in and launched by highly disenfranchised communities, bringing together very differently situated people who embody distinct forms of knowledge, housed inside and (more typically) outside the academy, to undertake systematic inquiry on issues of social (in)justice. These were not huge or well-funded research projects; they were humble and compelling inquiries rooted in everyday experiences of exploitation and the collective desire for radical alternatives. They sought to resuscitate what Edward Said (2012) called "lost causes" in communities that had been left behind by government policy and/or corporate expansion.

In Philadelphia and then in Atlanta, in the late 1890s and early 1900s, W. E. B. Du Bois collaborated with community members, elites, writers, journalists, and a theater troupe, mapping the systematic conditions in which poor Blacks were managing impossible lives, meticulously documenting how the problems that coagulated in the Black community, "the Negro problem," could be traced back to history, structures, and policies of exclusion and discrimination. Du Bois initiated study groups and careful environmental mapping initiatives; published in academic and popular outlets; authored a novel, *The Quest of the Silver Fleece* (1911/2008); and produced an extravagant pageant, *The Star of Ethiopia*, to educate the African American public about their history and sociology.

In 1889 in Chicago, sociologist Jane Addams and her partner Ellen Starr established Hull House as the first settlement house in the United States for recently arrived immigrants living collectively with Addams's and Starr's elite friends. In this center for research, study, and debate conducted across class and life stations, residents of Hull House collaboratively investigated truancy, typhoid, midwifery, housing, garbage collection, and cocaine use. Hull House initiated the research with/by residents, including elite women and poor immigrants, hosted popular education and discussion groups, and, like Du Bois, launched a drama club and theater group.

Across the Atlantic, in Marienthal, Austria, when the looms in the textile factory stopped in 1930, Maria Jahoda and colleagues from the Institute of Psychology at the University of Vienna joined with community members to document the material and embodied consequences of massive unemployment on community life. Like Du Bois and Addams before them, they published popular and academic texts, translating the research into materials for political organizers, and participating in a Socialist radio program, after which Jahoda was briefly imprisoned (Jahoda, Lazarsfeld, & Zeisel, 2001).

In Appalachia in the 1960s, Myles Horton, director of the Highlander Folk School/Research and Education Center in Tennessee, collaborated with sociologist Helen Lewis, Director of Appalachian Research at Berea College. They invited poor White housewives who were already collecting incidence records of fathers, husbands, and sons with black lung disease, to bring their citizen science together with disabled miners, black-lung physicians, leaders of the United Mine Workers, and musicians, to document, in epidemiology and song, the embodied consequences of the coal mining industry. The Highlander School was attacked by the Ku Klux Klan and padlocked shut by the FBI, only to reopen shortly thereafter, having received a bank loan from one of the few Black bankers in the Knoxville region.

In 1982, social psychologist and Jesuit priest Ignacio Martín-Baró returned from graduate School at the University of Chicago to El Salvador to initiate a series of "the people's" research projects at Universidad Centroamericana, where he was the Director of the University Institute for Public Opinion. "Nacho," as he was called, argued that participatory research, of and by "the people," was essential to "challenge the official lies" of the dictatorship. After a highly successful and yet extremely short career as a critical social researcher, on November 16, 1989, Martín-Baró, with five colleagues, their housekeeper, and her teenage daughter, were brutally murdered by a counter-insurgency unit of the Salvadoran government elite, a unit created at the U.S. Army's School of the Americas 9 years earlier. In his short career, Martín-Baró seeded and launched a line of liberation psychology, by and for the people.

While he was committed to publishing only in Spanish for his communities, and refused to be complicit in the fetish of English scholarly publications, his brilliant and inspiring writings on critical participatory research have been translated, and are available in *Writings for a Liberation Psychology: Ignacio Martín-Baró* (1994) (see also Lykes, 2012; Lykes & Coquillon, 2009, on liberation psychology in contexts of war and post-conflict).

During this same era, in the late 1980s, the Center for NuLeadership coalesced within the Greenhaven Think Tank, at Greenhaven prison in New York State. A research team of men in the prison, led by former Black Panther Eddie Ellis, was dedicated to investigating and preventing the rising numbers of Black and Latino men consigned to the New York State prison system. Under the direction of Ellis, who was imprisoned for 23 years, and with the help of psychologist Kenneth Clark, the men of the center—all incarcerated "street penologists"—designed a study that systematically determined that 85% of the New York state prisoners were Black and Latino, and 75% of them originated in seven neighborhoods downstate. From within the prison, members of the blacks' Resurrection Study group and the Latino-based group Conciencia integrated the Seven Neighborhood results into a Greenhaven Think Tank (1997) policy document. They urged a nontraditional policy analysis of the seven "symbiotic neighborhoods"—Lower East Side, South Bronx, Harlem, Brownsville, Bed/Sty, East New York, and South Jamaica—to the then 62 state prisons. The policy document recommended a nontraditional vision: that these men, while in prison, should be trained in community development, mentorship, and adult education, and once paroled back to those communities, should be funded to help rebuild the community through internships, mentoring, and community programs. The men even detailed their vision for a prisoner-run model prison. While Ellis has since passed away, the center survives in Brooklyn, and the soul of the center, like much of the leadership in the seven neighborhoods, can be found in cohorts of men and women formerly involved in what they call the "criminal punishment" system.

In 2012 a group of mothers and grandmothers in the South Bronx, working with a public interest lawyer, contacted social psychologists Brett Stoudt, María Elena Torre, and others at the Public Science Project (PSP) at The Graduate Center, CUNY (Stoudt & Torre, 2014). For years the women had been gathering evidence—videotaping, with their phones, out their windows—of the brutal interactions of the New York City Police Department (NYPD) with their sons; trading views from varied floors in their apartment buildings; archiving and analyzing the patterns; following their friends to the police station to "prove" their boys' innocence. Now they were asking for help to develop a more systematic community-wide survey. The Morris Justice Project, a deeply rooted community survey of aggressive policing in a 40-square-block area of the Bronx, gathered empirical evidence from more than 1,000 residents on overpolicing and the consequences for children, community safety, and democracy. The findings were introduced as legal evidence into the stop-and-frisk *Floyd v. City of New York* case, have been shared with the Communities United for Police Reform, and have been replicated by young people in the community group Make the Road in Brooklyn. The research team of mothers, grandmothers, community members, and researchers from the Graduate Center has presented their findings at the White House conference on Citizen Science (under Obama), to police departments in Toronto and Paris, and at a variety of academic meetings. They shared their work throughout the Bronx and Brooklyn, with the mayor's office, and in advocacy campaigns. As a team they facilitate Stats 'N Action workshops at the Yankee Tavern for community people to get familiar with local policing statistics, hold Know Your Rights sessions, and distribute cleverly designed fliers of their findings at Yankee Stadium. The T-shirts they distribute are tagged with open-ended survey responses that read, "It's not a crime to be who I am" or "Why do I always fit the description?" The shirt is most sobering in child's size Small.

In 2016, the People's Knowledge Editorial Collective in the United Kingdom—activists and refugee youth from NOMAD (Nations of Migration Awakening the Diaspora)—organized a volume that contests the hegemony of academic knowledge, the White gaze, and corporate-influenced research. Open access, online work reveals the wisdom of inquiry produced by and for refugee communities contending with global capitalism, migration, anti-Black violence, and what it means to be "settled" in a nation not quite one's own.

Across all the projects just described, we can trace a line of popular insurgent research—a deep strain and long history of everyday people gathering data on how they have been discriminated against, exposed to environmental toxins, imprisoned and aggressively policed—with the goals of informing policy, organizing communities, making films and music, and rebuilding active democratic communities across borders. (For a fantastic contemporary set of essays on critical community-based research, see Massey & Barreras, 2013; for transnational work on feminism and liberation psychology, see Lykes & Moane, 2009; and for education/youth based critical PAR, see Cammarota & Fine, 2008.)

In each research setting, challenging questions emerge about expertise, objectivity, and validity; sacred silences and suppressed "data"; Whiteness, privilege, and the colonial legacy of social science in communities of color; the tenuous relation of science and advocacy; the delicacies and ethics of legitimacy; and the vulnerability when academic researchers and community members link arms to cross dangerous power lines. In many of these cases, the stakes were high: Martín-Baró and the "murdered scholars" of UCA were brutally killed, some went to jail, research centers were closed, some researchers were intimidated by the state or lost funding, and mothers had their children harassed by the police. And yet these projects raise crucial questions about policy born in the collaborative wisdom of the margins, about critical knowledge production and democratic possibilities, about inquiry tied to action for justice and recognition. For a critical self-reflective look, I turn now to a few participatory projects taken up at the Public Science Project, at The Graduate Center, CUNY.

THE PUBLIC SCIENCE PROJECT

For the past 20 years, the Public Science Project at The Graduate Center, CUNY, has been organized as a hub for critical researchers, activists, policymakers, and then everyday people (of course we are all everyday people) making science and policy about the issues that plague their communities (Torre, Fine, Stoudt, & Fox, 2012). With María

Elena Torre as director, the signature of the Public Science Project is visible in the deeply participatory ethic that defines our work, conducting research with communities for transforming policy, supporting local campaigns, and theory building. When high school pushouts design studies of educational justice with educators, principals, researchers, and lawyers; when undocumented immigrant women who have experienced domestic violence join social workers, lawyers, and psychologists in shaping the research questions to provide meaningful options for survivors; when formerly incarcerated college students collaborate with university researchers, staff, and faculty to consider admissions policies attentive to access and security, and to document "The Gifts They Bring to the Universities"; when youth and elders collaborate with lawyers and social psychologists to put together a survey of relations with police in the Yankee Stadium area; when formerly incarcerated "long-termers" interrogate the question "How Much Punishment is Enough?" (Marquez-Lewis et al., 2013)— we recognize a wide range of ways to be experts. Together we work toward the "strong objectivity," as described by philosopher of science Sandra Harding (1994), which we believe strengthens the validity of and lifts up stories of complexity, ambivalence, and contradiction that deserve to be theorized, and by so doing, enhances the theoretical and provocative generalizability and sustainability of the work. Rooted in the ethic of "No research on us, without us" generated by disability rights activists, HIV activists, and indigenous communities, our projects are also designed with humility. We reflect on our internal dynamics of power; on who is made vulnerable as a consequence of the inquiry or the findings; on how we navigate the "choques"/conflicts (Anzaldúa, 1987; Torre & Ayala, 2009) that plague projects launched across dangerous power lines within the research team, funders, and policymakers; on how the work might be co-opted and to whom we are accountable.

This second half of this chapter sketches two projects launched out of PSP—both developed with commitments to critical participatory research, and a desire to "flip the script" by community researchers who "refuse to be the problem." These projects rest on Du Bois's (1904) still resonant question from more than a century ago:

> Between me and the other world there is ever an unasked question: unasked by some through feelings of delicacy; by others through the difficulty of rightly framing it. All, nevertheless, flutter round it. They

approach me in a half-hesitant sort of way, eye me curiously or com-
passionately, and then, instead of saying directly, How does it feel to be
a problem? they say, I know an excellent colored man in my town; or, I
fought at Mechanicsville; or, Do not these Southern outrages make your
blood boil? At these I smile, or am interested, or reduce the boiling to a
simmer, as the occasion may require. To the real question, "How does it
feel to be a problem"? I answer seldom a word. (pp. 1–2)

Below we consider how the production of knowledge shifts when
the people who are assumed to be the traditional "problem" are among
those who design the research so that histories, structures, and dynamics of exploitation are as visible as the bodies that "carry" the debris
of oppression and those who are privileged by the same. The projects
reviewed in this chapter draw from a range of research collaborations
of the Public Science Project (publicscienceproject.org), where we take
seriously Ignacio Martín-Baró's (1994) call for research that challenges
what he considered *official lies*.

We begin each project with W. E. B. Du Bois's (1904) question,
How does it feel to be a problem?, and investigate the structures and historic conditions that produce inequity and insert "problems" into the
bodies and communities under siege, whereby prevailing logic suggests, then, that "they" caused the problem, obscuring the face that
"they" embody the consequences of structural injustice. Our projects
interrogate how ascriptions of blame, responsibility, deficit, terror, or
damage adhere to some bodies, while other bodies, privileged bodies, appear laminated in a kind of Teflon. Our research teams include
those who have paid the most serious price for injustice sitting alongside other community members, advocates, policymakers, and more
traditionally trained researchers; together we practice what Harding
(1994) described as *strong objectivity*. That is, we build initially fragile
and increasingly sturdy contact zones where diverse knowledges dialogue, drawing on the language of Mary Louise Pratt (1991), developed further as an epistemological project by María Elena Torre (see
Torre & Ayala, 2009). We catalogue and pool our varied and dissenting
experiences and literacies: what we have experienced, read, seen, and
witnessed, and what we embody. We share, beckoning back to Paulo
Freire (1970), how we each "read the world" and then we stitch together a set of common questions for documenting the consequences
of privilege and oppression, revealing their predatory relationship,
and for unearthing stories untold.

Whether in prisons, schools, communities, or social movements, each PSP project opens with a "research camp," where those who most intimately carry the stories of injustice in their souls engage in critical dialogue with community-based practitioners, researchers, activists, youth, and educators. We share our provisional and partial knowledges, interrogate our differences, return awkwardly and deliberately to the fault lines of power within the group, dive into privilege and "choques"—difficult discussions (Torre & Ayala, 2009). In those conversations we deconstruct and sharpen our key constructs and catalogue the specificity of context. We interrogate the dominant story being circulated, unravel the discursive framing of the problem, and dig into the structures and ideologies of privilege that sustain inequities. We stay close to the messy grounds where the heavy footprints of policy can be found on historically silenced and bruised bodies. With mistakes, hiccups, awkward moves across fault lines of power, race, class, and position, we work to democratize the right to research (Appadurai, 2006), and by so doing, we strengthen the construct, context, and impact validity of our projects (Fine, 1994, 2006).

We call this practice Critical Participatory Action Research (CPAR). It is an epistemology, not a methodology. We engage in ethnography, large-scale secondary analysis of official databases and large-scale community surveys, interviews, focus groups, mapping, archival analyses, and various aesthetic methods. At base, critical PAR recognizes that expertise is widely distributed but legitimacy is not; that those who have experienced injustice have a particularly acute understanding of the affects, capillaries, consequences, and circuits of dispossession and privilege, like my mother Rosie from the bedroom and Du Bois from behind the veil.

What is distinct, and perhaps to some most jarring about CPAR, is that it privileges the line of vision marinated at the bottom of social hierarchies, not exclusively but fundamentally. Those who have been marginalized are central to framing the "problem," shaping research questions, defining the methods, crafting the instruments, determining samples, analyzing the material, designing products to be of use, and in the end, "owning" the data.

Many of our projects are rooted in deep collaboration with community members who have been defined as "the problem"—either the cause of or the site in which social problems become legible. People who live in high-crime neighborhoods, those who have been incarcerated, queer youth entangled with the juvenile justice system, Muslim Americans, (un)documented immigrants, and school pushouts have been (mis)represented as the source, rather than a consequence, of structural inequalities.

Post-colonial theorist Sylvia Wynter (2003) writes on and contests what she calls the Archipelago of Human Otherness, where "expert" and the most disenfranchised sit on opposing anchors of the archipelago. Her work challenges how we think about knowledge production, about who is positioned as the expert, about who is framed as the problem, about the standard against which Others will be compared. She documents historically how the concepts Man/normal/rational/free have always and essentially been juxtaposed against Other/subhuman/irrational/savage/immoral, in religion, law, education, and social science. This predatory relation carries a longstanding, perverse hierarchy of knowing versus being known.

Critical PAR inverts or queers this binary. The traditional "object" of research, way out on the edge of the Archipelago of Otherness—the young person assaulted by aggressive policing, the woman serving time in a maximum security prison, the gender-nonconforming young person pushed out of home and school—sits on the research team, reading theory across generations, debating frames, designing research, analyzing data, and curating products of meaning and use to policy, organizing, community life, and social theory. When flattened objects of scrutiny become subjects, theorists, researchers, and analysts, the research project makes visible how unevenly history and structures distribute resources, opportunities, and dignity, and reveals how communities of privilege benefit from and reproduce unjust arrangements. When research teams marinate very distinct forms of knowledge, we grow painfully aware of how social inquiry has historically been positioned from privileged grounds and has produced "findings" that naturalize unjust social relations (e.g., see Cahill, Quijada Cerecer, & Bradley, 2010). As Boaventura de Sousa Santos suggests in *Epistemologies of the South*: "Viewed from the perspective of the excluded and discriminated against, the historical record of global capitalism, colonialism, and patriarchy is full of institutionalized, harmful lies" (2014, p. viii).

We consider below two multisited CPAR projects focused on "institutionalized, harmful lies" that sustain educational (in)justice across districts, nations, and communities—to reflect on how participatory laboratories of critical knowledge production transform when those who have been objectified by traditional scholarship participate fully and critically in shaping, analyzing, publishing, and performing the evidence. (For full descriptions of the projects, see the sources cited.)

ECHOES OF *BROWN*: DOCUMENTING THE
UNFULFILLED PROMISE OF EDUCATIONAL INTEGRATION

Now I'd like you to look at the suspension data, and notice that
Black males in high schools were twice as likely as White males to be
suspended, and there are almost no differences between Black males
and Black females. But for Whites, males are three times more likely to
be suspended than females: 22% of Black males, 19% of Black females,
11% of White males and 4% of White females.

—Kareem Sergent

Kareem Sergent, an African American student attending a desegregated high school, detailed the racialized patterns of school suspensions to his largely White teaching faculty. Despite the arms crossed
in the audience, he continued: "You know me, I spend a lot of time in
the discipline room. It's really almost all Black males." Hesitant nods
were followed by immediate explanations about how in June, "it gets
Whiter," and "sometimes there are White kids, maybe when you're
not there." Kareem turned to the charts projected on the screen, "You
don't have to believe me, but I speak for the hundreds of Black males
who filled out this survey. We have to do something about it."

"Echoes of *Brown*" was a 13-school participatory project interrogating the "unfulfilled promise" of *Brown v. Board of Education*, the 1954
Supreme Court decision rendering segregation unlawful (for a full description of the project, see Fine, Roberts, et al., 2004). Our quantitative and qualitative research project was designed by and about diverse
students who attend desegregated high schools in the suburbs of New
York City and yet, for the most part, participate in classrooms segregated by race/ethnicity and class; who experience disciplinary practices
in ways quite disparate by race, class, and gender; who are assigned
to Special Education in ways that are overdetermined by race, class,
and gender. As a research collective of students and adults, diverse
by race, (dis)ability, school, academic passions, and perspectives, we
gathered data from almost 10,000 students in 13 districts; interviewed
scores of young people from various platforms or tracks within their
schools; and ultimately presented the data back to schools, as Kareem
was doing above. We performed the arc of the story, with spoken-word
poetry, dance, and interviews with courageous elders to an audience
of more than 500 on the 50th anniversary of *Brown v. Board* in 2004.

Kareem, a senior, was asking his faculty for nothing less than respect and a sense of belonging. Now meet Kendra Urdang, a young

White student, a junior also attending a public desegregated high school, who writes with passion and conviction about the racial imbalances that characterize her suburban high school:

> and in the classrooms, the imbalance is subtle,
> undercurrents in hallways.
> AP (Advanced Placement) classes on the top floor,
> special ed. in the basement.
> and although over half the faces in the yearbook
> are darker than mine, on the third floor,
> everyone looks like me.
> so it seems glass ceilings are often concrete.
>
> so let's stay quiet,
> ride this pseudo-underground railroad,
> this free ticket to funding from the board of ed.
> racism is only our problem if it makes the front page.
> although brown faces fill the hallways,
> administrators don't know their names,
> they are just the free ticket to funding,
> and this is not their school.

Gathering to Share Knowledges: Opening Echoes

In the fall of 2001, a group of suburban school superintendents of desegregated districts gathered to discuss the disaggregated Achievement Gap data provided by the states of New Jersey and New York. As is true nationally, in these desegregated districts, the test score gaps between Asian American, White American, African American, and Latino students were disturbing. Eager to understand the roots and remedies for the gaps, Superintendent Sherry King of Mamaroneck, New York, invited me (Michelle) and colleagues from The Graduate Center to join the research team. We agreed on the condition that we could collaborate with a broad range of students from suburban and urban schools to create a multiyear participatory action research project.

Over the course of 3 years of youth inquiry, through a series of research camps, more than 100 youth from urban and suburban high schools in New York and New Jersey joined researchers from The Graduate Center, CUNY, to study youth perspectives on racial and class based (in)justice in schools and the nation. We worked in the schools long enough to help identify a core of youth drawn from all corners of the school to serve as youth researchers—from special education, English as a Second Language, the Gay/Straight Alliances, discipline rooms, Student Councils, and advanced placement classes. We designed a multigenerational, multidistrict, urban-suburban database of youth and elder experiences, tracing the history of struggle for desegregation from *Brown* to date and social science evidence of contemporary educational opportunities and inequities analyzed by race, ethnicity, and class (Fine, Roberts, et al., 2004; Fine, Bloom, et al., 2005).

At our first session—an overnight retreat with 40-plus high schoolers at a Jesuit college where we launched our "research camp"—the youth from six suburban high schools and three urban schools immediately challenged the frame of the research: "When you call it an achievement gap, that means it's our fault. The real problem is an opportunity gap—let's place the responsibility where it belongs—in society and in the schools." And so we changed the name from the Achievement Gap Project to the Opportunity Gap Project.

Building Collective Capacities and Designing the Survey

Each research camp was held for 2 days at a time in a community and/or university setting. Deconstructing who can do research, what constitutes research, and who benefits, students were immersed in methods training and social justice theory. The students learned how to conduct interviews, focus groups, and participant observations; to design surveys and organize archival analyses. They listened to speakers who discussed the history of race and class struggles in public education. Many students received high school credits (when a course on participatory research was offered in their schools), and 42 received college credit for their research work.

At the first research camp we held scavenger hunts to highlight the distinct wisdoms each young person imported into the project. We watched a film on educational inequities, paused at key moments, and everyone wrote questions they would pose to make public the unique analytic lens that each contributed to the work. Young people drew maps of their schools—spaces where they felt they belonged, felt alienated, felt challenged, and felt ignored. It was clear that even within the same building, students were having very different experiences by race, class, ethnicity, and "achievement" levels.

Over the course of the weekend, we sketched out a survey to assess high school students' views of Race and Class (In)Justice in Schools and the Nation. The youth researchers were given a rough draft of the survey, including "open" sections of the survey—items we expect will be challenged and clarified, which is why we called it the "wrong draft"—and they dedicated the weekend to its revision, inserting cartoons, open-ended questions like, "What's the most powerful thing a teacher has said to you?" and sensitive Likert scale items such as "Sometimes I think I'll never make it" or "I would like to be in advanced classes, but I don't think I'm smart enough." Over the next few months, we translated the survey into Spanish, French-Creole, and Braille, and distributed it to 9th- and 12-graders in 13 urban and suburban districts. At the second and third camp, another group of youth researchers from the same schools (with some overlap) analyzed the qualitative and quantitative data from 9,174 surveys, 24 focus groups, and 32 individual interviews with youth.

Across the 3 years, we studied the history of Brown v. Board of Education, Emmett Till, Ella Baker, Jim Crow, Bayard Rustin, finance inequity, tracking, battles over buses and bilingualism, the academic success of the small schools movement, new schools for lesbian/gay/bisexual/transgender students, the joys, the dangers, and the unfulfilled promises of integration. We read about the growth of the prison-industrial complex at the expense of public education, and we reviewed how, systematically, federal policy has left so many poor and working-class children behind. As we worked with youth to map the contours of historic and contemporary racial struggle in schools, they interviewed elders in the Northeast, including Judge Jack Weinstein, who worked with Thurgood Marshall; Roscoe Brown, Jr., a Tuskegee Airman and civil rights leader; poet and activist Sonia Sanchez; and the amazing radical lawyer Arthur Kinoy. They held discussions with many who had been active in Black Panthers, Young Lords, the women's movement, and the disability-rights movement. They visited organizing groups and developed the skills to be youth researchers, advocates, and organizers in the campaign for fiscal equity, the struggle against high-stakes testing, and the fight for racially integrated, de-tracked classrooms.

Together we created an empirical map of the Racial and Class (In)Justices in secondary public schools across 13 districts. We disaggregated and analyzed data from the large-scale survey moving across suburban and urban schools and also rich material from a set of local mini-research projects. We visited each other's schools, documenting structures and policies that produce inequity and those spaces within schools and communities in which educators and youth have joined to create extraordinary collaborations, despite the odds. We wrote scholarly and popular articles, delivered professional and neighbor-hood talks. We traveled the nation to gather insights, to listen to young people, and to provoke policy, practice, and change with our research.

Critical Participatory Analysis:
Tracing Racialized Patterns of Inequity

Our research, conducted across some of the wealthiest and poorest schools in the nation, confirms what others have found: A series of well-established policies and practices assure and deepen the gap. The more separate America's schools are racially and economically, the more stratified they become in achievement. In our empirical reports on these data we refer to these ongoing sites of policy struggle as Six Degrees of Segregation:

1. Urban/suburban finance inequity
2. The systematic dismantling of desegregation
3. The racially coded tracking that organizes most desegregated schools
4. Racialized experiences of respect and supports in schools
5. Racialized and classed consequences of high-stakes testing
6. Highly racialized patterns of suspensions and disciplinary actions (for details of the findings, see Fine, Roberts, et al., 2004)

During 2003 we conducted many feedback sessions in schools, pre-senting racial patterns from the full database, and then school-specific trends (like the opening scene with Kareem) in the suburban commu-nities circling New York City, and we presented our material to groups of educators and policymakers throughout the country. But we met far too many adults who refused to hear and honor young people's com-plex renderings of *Brown*'s victories and continuing struggles. And so in the summer of 2003, with the anniversary of *Brown* approaching, we launched the Social Justice and the Arts Institute.

We brought together a diverse group of 13 young people, ages 13–21, who came from wealth and poverty and the middle; communi-ties in the suburbs surrounding New York City and within the city; Advanced Placement classes and Special Education classrooms. We joined Christians, Jews, Muslims, and youth with no religious affilia-tion; those of European, African, Caribbean, Palestinian, Latino, and blended ancestries. Some of the young people were headed for the

Ivy League, and some had spent time in juvenile facilities. We recruited youth interested in writing, performing, and/or social justice from youth groups and public schools to join with community elders, social scientists, spoken-word artists, dancers, choreographers, and a video crew. This group collectively pored through data from the Educational Opportunity Gap Project and learned about the legal, social, and political history of segregation and integration of public schools. The outcome was the creation of "Echoes," a performance of poetry and movement. Interviews with a series of elders who had been active in the Civil Rights Movement were spliced between the spoken word performances of the youth. In an empirical/performance experiment that bridged over time, geography, culture, and generation, we plaited political history, personal experience, research, and knowledge gathered from two generations building lives on both sides of *Brown*. To mark the 50th anniversary of the court decision, we performed "Echoes of *Brown*" for an audience of more than 500.

As a culminating product, we published a book/DVD of the work (Fine, Roberts, et al., 2004). The DVD included all the elder interviews and youth-spoken words, a video about the Social Justice and the Arts Institute, a summary of the research, and detailed commentary by the adult and youth researchers and educators working on educational justice in desegregated schools.

Fast Forward . . . by a Decade

Today, more than a decade later, schools in the United States are more segregated than in the past; disciplinary disparities and special education differentials by race and class persist. Many of the young people of Echoes stay in touch and are engaged in activist projects. Two married and gave birth to a baby they named Poet. The issues we were tackling—all manifestations of severely inequitable educational opportunities—remain stubbornly persistent. The project created a small rupture in 13 schools for telling a different story, one that is now being animated by activist educators, parents, community members, and students (see Journey for Justice Alliance, 2013). They are struggling for educational justice in desegregated and segregated buildings; freedom from high-stakes testing; finance equity; restorative justice in place of highly criminalized suspensions of predominantly young men of color and gender-nonconforming young women; and decolonizing of the curriculum. The struggle for just education continues in this nation and globally.

DO YOU BELIEVE IN GENEVA?
CRITICAL PARTICIPATORY ACTION RESEARCH
WITH THE GLOBAL RIGHTS CAMPAIGN

Committed to the transnational mapping of educational exclusion, Global Partners for Educational Justice sponsored the Amplifying Youth Voices on Rights, Poverty and Discrimination Project, to support young activists from marginalized ethnic communities to evaluate international compliance with the Dakar Framework for Action on achieving the Education For All (EFA) goals, particularly goal 2: "ensuring that by 2015 all children, particularly girls, children in difficult circumstances and those belonging to ethnic minorities, have access to and complete, free and compulsory primary education of good quality."

The Public Science Project (specifically Eve Tuck, Sarah Zeller-Berkman, and me) was invited to help the young people collaboratively create a bottom-up survey that could travel respectfully across very different communities to determine levels of discrimination and obstacles to education that are

- Accessible (regarding transportation, e.g., or the existence of local practices that disallow members of certain castes, colors, genders, religions, tribes to attend school)
- Free (are there fees for school, books, uniforms, travel?)
- Complete (how many years of education are available?)
- Of quality (are there adequate books, supports, desks, bathrooms, qualified educators, culturally sensitive and responsive curricula, meaningful assessments, not just tests that punish?)

In each community, focus groups would be conducted to gather local stories of varying levels of access to educational opportunities. Global Rights would collect the material from across meridians, and some of the young people would speak back, armed with research, to the UN Commission on Human Rights in Geneva, Switzerland. Then each of these young activists would return to their homes and create a participatory research team there, in order to produce a video, brochure, or website representing local issues of educational access. (For a full description of the project, see Fine, Tuck, & Zeller-Berkman, 2007.)

Challenging Constructs and Measures
of Global Educational Discrimination

As we tried to construct an instrument that could travel the globe, we confronted key challenges of method that haunt any design, particularly one that yearns to stretch globally, and also put down roots locally. The most palpable tension could be felt in the distinct goals of global and local work. A collective desire to be heard and to affect public policy saturated the training session: To varying degrees, we all knew this was really important for young people to gather together across continents and build a movement for educational justice, bolstered by statistics and testimonies about the global blades of domination. At the same time, the air thickened in an unspoken dialect, fuming in each of us: How will this help my people, my community, my family? Tensions of North vs. South; Indigenous, undocumented, refugee and immigrant; the imperial presence and terror exported by the United States and the United Kingdom seasoned the air, unspoken, as we sat together, with bagels and cream cheese, under the Manhattan Bridge in Brooklyn, NY.

The young people in the room, our co-researchers, embodied incredibly rich, complex, and diverse histories, came from a range of contexts, and were engaged in local campaigns around youth and education. The idea that we could come up with a common framework for measuring educational discrimination seemed, at once, exhilarating and nuts.

The more we talked, the more we realized that concepts like "discrimination," clear in law, were diffuse in everyday life. Once we heard about life as lived in *real* towns, barrios, fields, cities, communities, and kitchens, we recognized that the ripples of globalized oppression take varied forms—alcoholism, domestic violence, hopelessness, indigency—none easily reduced to a simple descriptor of discrimination. We had to shovel down into the sands of local places to understand how discrimination is lived.

The Stubborn Particulars of the Local

By day three, we were "modeling" a focus group, the kind these young people might facilitate with youth back home in order to generate a map of deeply contextualized, situated stories of discrimination, denial of access, obstacles encountered, and resiliencies displayed by youth in their communities.

It was in the focus group that some key issues were voiced. Five participants (from Nepal, Tanzania, India, Cameroon, and Algeria) were asked to draw maps of their travels from childhood to present, through schooling; to identify significant places, emotions, relationships, and struggles; to specify the obstacles they encountered; and to detail the people and movements that supported them. One chair was left empty for anyone in the "outer circle" to join us. The problematics of globalizing hope through research poured into the group like lava. The pain of everyday life inside long histories of colonialism, abuse, and injustice could no longer be denied. The existential question of "proof"—will they ever listen?—whispered in all of our ears.

There was, of course, an important project underway—to work deep and wide, to insist that Geneva listen. And yet throughout the room, like waves of hope and despair, we could read faces asking,

- Will this matter back home?
- Do self-doubts count as the last drop of oppression and discrimination?
- How are the fists and the slaps of a father accounted for in a human rights campaign for education?
- Should we consult the elders in our community about the work?
- If we consult the elders, will they shut down the conversations of the young people?

We realized that very different theories of change were operating unspoken in the room, and so we posed the question "What are your visions for educational justice?" While Tano, a Roma student from Bulgaria, complained that Roma children "only have Roma educators and other Roma in their schools," others wanted to be educated by, and with, people who "come from my community." Some wanted to be prepared to attend "elite" secondary and higher education institutions, others—particularly Indigenous activists—were fighting for culturally responsive schools, where native language would be spoken, and decolonialized histories would be taught. Some wanted to be educated "with all kinds of students and teachers," while others wanted local, culturally sensitive, and immersed education. Some demanded access to English as liberatory; others viewed English as imperialistic. Some come from places that have no schools for miles; some have only seasonal teachers; some are segregated but want to be with "others"; some are "integrated" and yearn for a space of their own. Some trusted contact with dominant groups, and many didn't.

As the stories filled the room, the whispers grew louder: "Access to what?" Do we all want the same thing? Do we all really seek access to a Western—"free, complete, quality"—education?

"Good Enough" Constructs
That Could Migrate Across Differences

We wanted to create a survey that could tap local dynamics but also translate across borders of nation-states and ethnic communities. We split into three groups. Eve met with one group that was working on creating survey questions that would assess obstacles to school access and completion. The group began by listing the reasons that, from their own lives or siblings' or friends' lives, students might not finish their studies. They quite easily arrived at a list of obstacles:

- It isn't safe for students to attend or travel to school.
- There are family issues and home issues that prevent students from attending.
- There is no reason or benefit or incentive for students to complete their schooling.
- Economic issues keep students working rather than attending school.
- The school language is different from the student's home language.
- The student or her family have physical or mental health issues.
- The student's culture clashes with the school culture.
- Religious issues prevent students from attending.
- The schools do not meet the students' needs (including needs having to do with language, gender, age, and ability).

The next step was more difficult. We wanted to generate a survey that could translate across wealth and poverty because we intended to survey elite and impoverished youth from each nation. We would translate the surveys, and then each young person would travel back home and administer the survey to 25 males and 25 females from the "dominant" group and 25 and 25 from the "marginalized" group.

We then dove into the morass of trying to define "dominant" or "privilege." We asked: "What does privilege look like in the Dominican Republic?"

Ivrance Martinez, born in Haiti, now living in the Dominican
   Republic: "They think they are white in their minds."
Varshaa Ayyar: But I'm having trouble with the other side of this
   idea—how do we identify who is marginalized in India? There
   are so many layers.
Tano added, "Are the Turkish immigrants in Bulgaria part of
   the dominant . . . since they too discriminate against us, the
   Roma?"

One member of the project, Sandra Carolina Rojas Hooker, a lawyer from Nicaragua, a Creole of African descent, acknowledged what so
many in the room were thinking, *"But really, so many of us are mixed, no?"*
   Elvia Duque, an Afro-Colombian lawyer, and President of the
Regional Coalition in Health for African Descendants in the Americas,
insisted that we think about how we ask people about race/ethnicity
because "so many deny their African heritage in self reports."
   And then someone whispered, loud enough for us to hear but not
notice who spoke, "What about those among us who collaborate with
those who want to oppress us: Are they dominants or marginalized?"
   These questions live at the core of human experience, at the nub
of struggles for justice, in the fault lines of community fractures, and
are usually ignored in conversations about survey design. Because
we were a participatory research team, these questions of difference,
power, privilege, and the inadequacy of categories would not be silenced; they sat in the very belly of the research.
   We decided, eventually, that we would not try to survey youth of
privilege. Most of the young people believed that privileged people
wouldn't stay in the room long enough to have a conversation; or
they wouldn't tell the truth; or they wouldn't take seriously research
by marginalized youth. We were sorry, however, because we never
want to separate "oppressed" from "privileged," and always must keep
in mind the predatory relation between the two.
   If operationalizing privilege was difficult, coming to a shared defi-
nition of discrimination was almost impossible. The global human
rights documents were extremely articulate about legal definitions of
discrimination, but the young people were equally persuasive about
how messy and inchoate discrimination is when it leaks into their
lives. In their maps and stories, many mentioned casually incidents
of family illness, death of a sibling or a father, a parent needing an
operation. Health tragedies were spray-painted all over the biograph-
ic journeys of poor youth trying to get educated. They detailed their

many returns home from college in order to nurse a family member back to health. We commented on the emotion in the room—how many lives, cultures, communities, and responsibilities these young people were carrying in their hearts and souls, in their backpacks as they traveled off to college; how heavy a burden, how joyous the support they transported in their bellies.

Varshaa spoke up again. She, more than anyone, had, for 2 days, carried and voiced the pain in the room, in the world, in the micropolitics of everyday life: "Please, I am not in the circle, but I would like to present my map. I think it will tell you much about my community." Her map tells the story of family violence within her Dalit community. "My father is Dalit—you know, what they call untouchable, and he can't get work; he drinks and beats my mother; I can't attend school because I am tending her wounds. Is that discrimination?" Varshaa's map illuminated how the slow, toxic drip feed of discrimination seeps into homes, families, peer relations, and bodies, and transforms.

Refusing Geneva/Sharing Evidence

A bit later in the training, ethical questions about participatory research and indebtedness, loyalty and betrayal began to fester, under the table, outside in the hallways, in quiet voices. We all understood that PAR is undertaken with and for the local community to incite protest, to insist on change. But when we shifted our focus to Geneva, asking the youth researchers to "jump scale," the anxieties of handing off our stories to the Human Rights Commission, and questions about obligation to whom, grew more intense. Images of audience and purpose blurred; fantasies of vulnerability and exploitation spiked.

At the very exhausting and exhilarating end of our 3 days together, Aliou from Cameroon spoke,

> You know, this isn't a criticism of the last few days, but I want
> to say that we might never get to Geneva. Even if we do, I don't
> think they believe in us. But I have grown so much, learned so
> much, being with all of you these last few days, listening to stories
> of young people fighting for justice in their own communities.
> Our relationships, our skills, that's what I'll take back to my
> community. But Geneva, I don't know that I believe in Geneva.

Aliou gave voice as others nodded, some whispered over cigarettes. Bold in his recognition that perhaps he doesn't believe in Geneva . . .

and perhaps they don't believe in him, Aliou refused to be what he called "a trophy" one more time in a human rights race. He was soon joined by others who argued that the work had to speak back to their home communities and mobilize local change.

The Global Rights project was an exercise in the critical production of radical evidence by powerful activists from marginalized communities. Ultimately the young people decided it was most important that the material be shared horizontally—across national borders, among youth activists—not necessarily to Geneva or other elites. As Aliou and many others have warned, evidence—even evidence generated by the people for the people—constitutes only one resource that must be brought to bear in a long, participatory march toward social justice. Linking across the globe, we stitched a humble, fragile solidarity among youth hungry for educational justice.

CRITICAL PARTICIPATORY ACTION RESEARCH: KNEADING, TRANSLATING, AND BRAIDING ACROSS AND WITHIN BORDERLANDS

> I am an act of kneading, of uniting and joining that not only has produced both a creature of darkness and a creature of light, but also a creature that questions the definitions of light and dark and gives them new meanings.
>
> —Gloria Anzaldúa, 1987, p. 103

Anzaldúa writes provocatively about the magic that materializes in moments between—mysteries that conjure when creatures of darkness meet creatures of light; new meanings born at jazzy and contentious borders and in tricky relationships. And she puts to words the labors and desires of critical PAR—to knead, unite, join, and give new meanings at the rich intersections of identities, cultures, histories, and struggles (see Collins, 1998; Crenshaw, 1995).

In times of sprawling global capitalism and rising White nationalism, as people hunker down into defensive corners of "sameness," inequality gaps widen and segregation becomes normative; fear permeates and anger leads; borders close and walls are built. In these divisive times, critical PAR carves a provisional and delicate space of kneading; a research complex that deliberately brings people together *to contend with our differences*, to design inquiries from the bottom and generate challenging knowledge from the margins. In critical PAR projects we furnish modestly fugitive spaces for critical knowledge production among community activists, researchers, artists, youth, and education workers. We curate inquiry in humble and humbling corners to explore the capillaries of structural violence and cultivate radical possibilities beyond our current horizons (see also Bhatia, 2007).

Multisited critical PAR has an even more ambitious stretch, toward generating critical knowledge both *in* and *across* places, engaging in what Boaventura de Sousa Santos (2014) calls "the work of translation" (see Cindi Katz on "counter-topographies," 2001). In addressing the World Social Forum, Santos argued that the Forum—a transnational political project

> holds out the hope that another world is possible . . . but reveals the diversity of social struggles fighting against neoliberal globalization . . . and calls for a giant work of translation . . . to build articulation, aggregation and coalition. (p. 15)

Multisited CPAR projects exercise the muscles of community building and knowledge production through articulation, aggregation, and coalition. By so doing, the cross-cutting blades of exclusion grow visible, and the sweet counter-hegemonic spaces of care, love, and radical possibility come to light.

As illustrated in the earlier descriptions of "Echoes of *Brown*" and the Global Rights Campaign, and in the next chapter of *"What's Your Issue?"*, multisited CPAR projects are particularly challenging and, frankly, thrilling. For all the ways these projects are fraught, never quite what we thought they would be, and always better than we imagined, multisite CPAR projects promote critical inquiry emanating from everyday people, seasoned with the wisdom of experience and mobilized by diverse coalitions for action in specific sites, and across others. In *Echoes*, youth researchers recruited from top "track" and special education classes worked together across wealthy and relatively impoverished districts. In the *Global Rights Campaign* activists collaborated from the Global North and South, from colonizing countries and Indigenous tribal lands.

By analyzing evidence across sites, we could discern what was stubbornly particular to a school/community/state/nation, and what could radiate—as dispossession and resistance (see Fine, 2012, on "whose evidence?"). For instance, in urban communities, where schools rely heavily on policing to manage discipline, racial suspension disparities spike, and yet in schools that refuse to administer high-stakes testing, these disparities shrink. In Indigenous communities, educational inadequacy and tracking are compounded by White-washed history curricula, and yet in small schools where community members and faculty collaborate on school design, cultural histories are built into the structure of academic life. While these regional particularities are crucial elements in local fights for educational justice, it is also true that young people are energized—ironically—to fight for educational justice when they "discover" that consistently, across communities, racial disparities can be found in access to advanced classes, enrollment in special education, and involvement with suspension; that girls, low-income youth, and darker youth are systematically denied educational access across nation states, and that LGBTQI young people of color are far more likely than White peers to report negative interactions with police, schools, peers, and families in every state in the nation. Multisited critical PAR projects make visible the coarse and enduring threads of oppression that carry across sites, and the vibrant threads of resistance that dot particular communities.

With a design commitment to ethnographic depth and quantitative and qualitative breadth, multisited critical PAR projects reveal systematic forces of structural injustice, flexible levers for change, and exceptional spaces mobilized against dominant flows, as irresistible as they may seem. These projects knead, as Anzaldúa implores (1987); they seek to translate, as de Sousa Santos (2014) argues, and they ignite a "wide awakeness" within the research collectives and the audiences fortunate enough to bear witness (Greene, 1977, p. 119).

And so we end this chapter with "much ado" about prepositions: In deeply troubling times, when research is designed and implemented *by/with*, rather than *on, for,* or *about* a relentlessly marginalized group of young people, everything changes: the energy and imagination; the theory, construct, method, sample, and analysis; our understandings of objectivity, subjectivity, validity; and the products we produce. When we work in intentional and often difficult collaboration within and across sites, unexpected insights and incites emerge from the animated and sometimes disruptive chorus of voices. When we work both *in* and *across places*, the sharp blades of oppression and the coarse ties of resistance grow apparent, but so do the delicious alternatives that represent vibrant possibilities of what might be. Critical PAR projects designed across communities/states/nations make visible our common struggles, our desires to "be of use" (Fine & Barreras, 2001), and our profound interdependence—all essential to sustaining our collective futures.

"Speaking Words of Wisdom"

Metabolizing Oppression into Intersectional Activism, Radical Wit, and Care Work

with María Elena Torre, David Frost, and Allison Cabana

In August 1897, in *The Atlantic Monthly*, William Edward Burghardt Du Bois published "The Strivings of the Negro People," in which he introduced the notion of double-consciousness:

> After the Egyptian and Indian, the Greek and Roman, the Teuton and Mongolian, the Negro is a sort of seventh son, born with a veil, and gifted with second-sight in this American world,—a world which yields him no true self-consciousness, but only lets him see himself through the revelation of the other world. It is a peculiar sensation, this double-consciousness, this sense of always looking at one's self through the eyes of others, of measuring one's soul by the tape of a world that looks on in amused contempt and pity. One ever feels his two-ness,—an American, a Negro; two souls, two thoughts, two unreconciled strivings; two warring ideals in one dark body, whose dogged strength alone keeps it from being torn asunder. (1904, p. 88)

The idea of double-consciousness faded over the century—at least in the academy—with Du Bois erased in an act of what Rabaka (2010) calls "Epistemological Apartheid." Sociologists including Erving Goffman and psychologists including Kenneth Clark rose to the interpretative apex to chronicle the consequences of stigma. In 1959, Goffman wrote, "We are all just actors trying to control and manage our public image, we act based on how others might see us" (p. 19). "Two-ness" grew muted in academic writings on oppression and stigma. Notions of resistance, refusal, rejection of assimilation were under-theorized, and replaced by notions of damage, deficit, internalization, conformity, and self-hatred (see Cross, 1991 for a brilliant contestation of the scholarly fetish with racialized "damage"). The question of "willful subjects," to borrow from Sara Ahmed (2014), to amplify those who have been colonized and betrayed and yet remain desiring and rebellious, deserves critical interrogation *by* and *with* those whose lives have been most severely marginalized by political economy and public institutions.

In 1988 Gayatri Spivak posed the question, "Can the subaltern speak?" In 2006 Arjun Appadurai argued for the "right to research." And in this chapter, in 2017, queer and trans youth of color not only speak; they research. They not only research their own conditions, but they speak back to the ideological and material forms of heteronormativity and homophobia, excessive accumulation of wealth at the top, racism, xenophobia, and misogyny that saturate the historic moment in which their adolescence/young adulthood unfolds. And so we find, Drs. Goffman and Clark, that these young people do not simply internalize or hate themselves (see Cross, 1991). Instead, they speak with multiple and critical consciousness, understanding well their willful subjectivities. They metabolize oppression into wounds indeed, but also radical wit, expansive activism, sanctuary relationships, and carework with Others (Luttrell, 2013).

COLONIALITY OF BEING

In his 2007 essay "On the Coloniality of Being," Nelson Maldonado-Torres, asks:

> What is the meaning of damné? The damné is the subject that emerges in a world marked by the coloniality of Being. . . . The damné is either invisible or excessively visible. The damné exists in the mode of not-being there, which hints at the nearness of death, at the company of death. . . . The appearance of the damné is not only of social significance but of ontological significance as well. It indicates the emergence of a world structured on the basis of the lack of recognition of the greater part of humanity as givers, which legitimizes dynamics of possession, rather than generous exchange. . . . obliterate[ing] the traces of the trans-ontological by actually giving birth to a world in which lordship and supremacy rather than generous interaction define social dynamics in society. (p. 259)

Borrowing from Maldonado-Torres, in all of our projects we pose the problematic question: How do those who have been damne(d) design critical participatory inquiry on structural violence, the collective and embodied consequences, complex lives navigating survival and resistance, and the radical possibilities for imagining another tomorrow?

As mentioned in Chapter 2, Leigh Patel (2016) calls for decolonizing research that decenters Whiteness, uproots the colonial genealogies, and dismantles the complicities of traditional research sutured to the stealing of land, dreams, opportunities, and stories. Maldonado-Torres (2007) also articulates the obligations of what he considers the decolonizing project in which dominant constructs are opened to interrogation, invitations are cast broadly to critique and dismantle ideas and material structures that sustain hierarchy, and historically silenced lines of analysis take center stage.

> For decolonization, concepts need to be conceived as invitations to dialogue and not as impositions. They are expressions of the availability of the subject to engage in dialogue and the desire for exchange. Decolonization in this respect aspires to break with monologic modernity . . . [interrogating] coloniality critically from different epistemic positions and according to the manifold experiences of subjects who suffer different dimensions of the coloniality of Being. (p. 261)

In this chapter we dive into a research project interrogating the consciousness and activism "stirring" today in LGBTQ+/GNC youth across the country. We sought to unpack how young people metabolize what Maldonado-Torres would call the "coloniality of being," as they embody and narrate a stunning blend of wounds, critique, wisdom, and creativity. This group has experienced a rupture in their social relations, and has been exiled by the scars of heteronormativity, and often racism. As you will see in the material presented below, some, like sacrificial trees in a forest blown by violent winds, fall—to rage and/or suicidal ideation. But most don't. Most yearn for, and some demand, complex recognition and an opportunity to engage justice projects larger than themselves. They engage critical research, they write, and they are producing a collective website at whatsyourissue.org.

QUEER YOUTH UNDER SIEGE: WHAT'S YOUR ISSUE?

Just as we were about to sit down for lunch to discuss the possibility of a large grant to the Public Science Project to launch a national participatory survey by and for LGBTQ youth of color, the foundation officers said to us, "Did you ever notice that the leaders of key youth movements, DREAMers, Education Justice, Immigration Justice, Black Lives Matter, Black Youth Project 100, Native youth, leaders of disability rights, spoken word poets . . . are disproportionately queer youth of color?"

A group of funders approached María Elena Torre, director of the Public Science Project, and Michelle, about the possibility of a national, participatory survey designed with LGBTQ youth of color. While LGBTQ youth research has focused primarily on depression, bullying, and suicide, sampling largely White, elite kids in gay-straight alliances (student-run clubs), these funders knew that gender-nonconforming, trans, and queer youth were disproportionately homeless, in foster care, and involved with juvenile justice, and that many young people find the binaries of gay/lesbian and heterosexual, as well as male and female, to be psychically violent *straight* jackets. They were interested in funding a national participatory project that could gather narratives and responses from a much more inclusive sample of queer, trans, and gender-nonconforming young people living at the margins, specifically those of color who might tell a different story about the desires, betrayals, dreams, demands, and radical imaginaries. And so in 2016 *What's Your Issue?* (WYI) was born, rooted in the recognition that, indeed, the stories of poor and working-class queer and trans youth needed to come out of the closet, and that research would be best shaped by and with the perspectives of those who have been most marginalized even within the movement for equality.

Building the Advisory Board

To ground ourselves in an expansive understanding of gender/sexuality/race, both within and across regions, we invited a very diverse— by geography, race/ethnicity, sexuality, gender expression, and lived experience—advisory board to sketch the design. (The *What's Your Issue?* project was launched by María Elena Torre and Michelle Fine and developed and supported by David Frost, Allison Cabana, Liz Carlin, Emerson Brisbon, Ejeris Dixon, Kyle Rapinan, Alex Melnick, Julieta Salgado, Samy Galvez, and over 200 multiracial LGBTQ+ and GNC youth and organizers nationwide.)

Board membership was half youth and half adults; members were nearly all LGBTQ+ and gender-nonconforming, most working at the intersections of racial/sexual justice, immigration and sexuality, disability and sexuality, from rural and urban areas, high schools and youth centers, foster care, and gay-straight alliances. We invited artists, activists, educators, researchers, and young people from across the country, and from organizations focused on LGBTQ+ issues, but also spoken word, immigration struggles, young people engaged with social media and public radio, squatting youth and DREAMers, young people in foster care, and those precariously housed.

We wanted *What's Your Issue?* to document the wide range of experiences, dreams, and desires of lesbian, gay, bisexual, trans, queer, plus, and gender-nonconforming youth, with a special emphasis on LGBTQ+ and GNC youth of color. We were moved by Sara Ahmed's volume, *Willful Subjects* (2014), in which she asks, "What would it mean to offer a queer history of will? Given that the will becomes a technique, a way of holding a subject to account, it could be understood as a *straightening* device." If we have this understanding of will—*as a charge against groups who won't straighten*—"we would not be surprised by its queer potential: after all, you only straighten what is already bent" (p. 8).

Democratizing Design:
Building a Critical National Participatory Survey

We set out to design the WYI survey with a blend of traditional youth survey items, and also an array of "homegrown" items, from urban and rural, the Northeast but also the South, West, and middle of the country. We offered small "gift cards" to subsidize "survey-making parties" across the country where young people generated survey themes and developed items. Eventually they edited the multiple drafts of the survey in Tucson, Seattle, rural Montana, New Orleans, Miami, and elsewhere. The final survey, distributed online, tapped issues of meaning, urgency, debate, desire, and controversy in the lives of LGBTQ+ and GNC youth in their communities, with traditional Likert scales and lots of creative, open-ended questions. A full copy of the final survey is available at whatsyourissue.org. As of this writing, we have only begun to scratch open our participatory analysis of the material.

To pilot what we call the "wrong draft" of the survey, cobbled from suggestions across the country, traditional surveys, and homegrown items, we put out a call for LGBTQIA+ and GNC youth in New York City to join us on the second floor of a Korean deli in midtown Manhattan. In August 2016, more than 150 young people (paid $15/hour for 4 hours) streamed into the deli, climbing the steps to the second floor, where the air was an acrid blend of air freshener, mildew, and perhaps a slight smell of chlorine/urine. We ate, laughed, traded pronouns, pseudonyms, and real names, and created and presented colorful banners for "what the world should know about LGBTQ youth." They split off into groups, for hours, to critique, edit, revise, and remix the "wrong draft" of the survey. Across rooms, groups, and arguments we critiqued, rewrote, and reassembled what would eventually become a national online survey filled with some standardized, but many more homegrown, questions about activisms and dreams, betrayals and worries, intersections and anxieties, gifts and dreams.

In a small room, 20 young people from various agencies, activist organizations, and educational areas met to discuss some of the more "contentious issues" that might reproduce some of the most damning stereotypes about LGBTQ/GNC youth—questions on pain, betrayal, needs, questions that could be misheard as pathologizing or damage oriented. We wanted to avoid, to the extent possible, what Thomas Teo (2010) would call "epistemological violence," that is, producing research that reinforces demonizing stereotypes. Long, difficult conversations ensued, with "lively" discussion and much dissensus about what to include, how to phrase questions, what to ask, and what not to ask.

"This survey is going out all over the country, and to Guam and Puerto Rico. One of the things we want to know is how young people experience injustice, how often, and how they cope." We explained that we wanted to build on research of Bruce McEwen (2000), who has documented how the neuroscience of injustice "gets under the skin" and makes us sick (as discussed in Chapter 4). "We are going to list a bunch of experiences in a column, that might be considered unfair or unjust, and respondents will rate how stressful they find these experiences. What kinds of things should we list?" Silence, and then a hand was raised.

Erica, self-defined as a Puerto Rican femme lesbian, a senior in high school, explained, "I am fine when I walk down the street alone; but when I'm with my girlfriend, police say, 'I want to fuck both of you.'" And you could hear fingers snapping all around us.

More hands:

- No place to live.
- My family threw me out.
- Finding out you are HIV positive and having your family tell you to leave.
- Not being able to afford transportation to get to work.

- When I just tap my girlfriend's nose in the hallway in school, or give her a quick kiss on the cheek, some security guard screams TOO MUCH PDA [public display of affection] when the straight kids are basically having sex on the other side of the hall—and my mother gets a call!
- Getting beat up in school, called a faggot, and I get suspended or transferred 'cause they say they can't promise to keep me safe.

And then Jay, whose preferred personal pronoun was "they," raised a hand, and from under a baseball cap sitting atop a full Afro, soft brown skin, welcoming smile, gray eyes, spoke, "Every time the police stop and frisk me, you know in parks or at the piers or even in my neighborhood, when they feel my breasts they get angry and beat me up. Can we put that on the survey?"

We spent two hours on how to ask about gender/sex categories. "Do we ask about sex assigned at birth?" Some applauded, and others yelled out, "That question is offensive!" After that, for an open-ended question, "What's your gender?" the survey offers a long list with CHECK ALL THAT APPLY. And another, "What's your sexuality?" To date, we have gathered almost 40 categories for each. Needless to say, this may be a thrilling moment for queer theory and the proliferation of gender/sexuality categories and identities, but an empirically awkward moment for survey construction. The point is not to "get it right," but to open the conversation to hear the myriad ways in which young people describe their genders, sexualities, and racial/ethnic identities, and to hear how fiercely they resist narrow categories and boxes.

On the Art of Sampling and (De)Constructing Categories

We closed the survey portal once we had sampled almost 6,000 young people, from every state in the nation, and from Puerto Rico and Guam. With extraordinary help from organizations across the nation working with youth in general, youth on the rim, and LGBTQ youth, our survey sample (at the time of this writing) includes 56% who identify as trans/nonbinary/gender nonconforming, 40% youth of color, 80% in school, 39.8% experiencing housing insecurity, and 23% who consider themselves to be religious. Our goal was to include the widest range of LGBTQIA/GNC youth possible, oversampling for youth of color and trans youth, with geographic spread. We make no claims to the sample being representative. Indeed, we think it is dubious that any "sample" of LGBTQIA/GNC youth can be, or should aspire to be, representative—but we are extremely pleased that the sample is so widely inclusive of so many who survive in the shadows of social policy and research.

With more than 6,000 respondents, who offered more than 20 gender categories, and more on the question of race/ethnicity, and with a 40-person youth research collective deeply critical of "categories," we worked hard to generate a process for how we would analyze the data; how we would create analytic comparisons; how we would collapse the data. While some of the young people would prefer that we tell 6,000 individual stories, we all understood that some merging of the data was needed. But each "collapse" felt like a paper cut on the soul of these respondents, who were so generous and explicit about all the complex identities they embody. We dedicated hours of labored dialogue, dissent, and negotiation in order to generate provisional agreements for the purpose of disaggregating the data by race/ethnicity and gender.

With a great debt to the difficult, deliberative, and delicate dialogues among the research collective, we rejected the normative social-science tradition of damage-based evidence, pointing to group-level differences as "disparities" that "stick" to some bodies and not others. However, working closely with youth activists in racial, sexual, and gender justice movements, we also could not ignore the devastating price young people pay for transgressing heteronormativity, and the consequences in their lives of racism and misogyny. We needed to document who is banished from families, exiled from church, abused by police, alienated in schools, exposed to violence on the streets and online.

The preliminary findings in this chapter tell three important counter-stories:

1. structural precarity in the form of housing and financial insecurity, food scarcity, aggressive policing, and alienating schools has serious adverse consequence on academic, physical, and psychological well-being, particularly for youth of color and trans/gender nonconforming youth;
2. although LGBTQ+/GNC young people narrate rich, complex, fluid, and multiple identities that are "beyond categories," structural violence bears down predictably and dramatically along the intersectional axes of race, ethnicity, gender, immigration status, region and sexuality. And yet . . .

3. LGBTQ+/GNC young people under siege indeed carry wounds of oppression, but they have an acute ability to metabolize discrimination into activism, speak words and wisdom of "radical wit," and extend enormous generosity to peers and other queer youth.

Critical Participatory Analysis: Understanding Structural Precarity

Lesbian, gay, bi, queer, and trans young people, particularly youth of color, are situated in and vulnerable to the mean edge of neoliberalism, austerity, and rising conservative assault on all things public, on people of color, the LGBTQ community, immigrants, indigenous people, and those living in poverty. We heard these concerns in the deli, under Obama, and now only more amplified under Trump.

To assess *how* structural conditions and dispossessions move under the skin of young people, we created a Precarity Index, assessing the extent to which youth report themselves to be unstably housed, experiencing financial or food insecurity, vulnerable to police, at risk of being pushed out of school, and/or worried about Immigration Control Enforcement (ICE).

On the precarity index, we found important, if unsurprising, group-level differences. Youth of color experience significantly more precarity than White youth ($p = .000$); trans/gender-nonbinary/gender-fluid youth experience significantly more precarity than cisgender youth ($p = .004$). Thus when researchers "find" differences by race/ethnicity or gender/sexuality, it is so important to contextualize and structuralize these differences; distinct "outcomes" derive in large part from real, structural conditions of discrimination, betrayal, exile, and moral exclusion from the political and affective economy of labor, schooling, housing, and family love—not from some "demographic fantasy" about the group itself.

Further, while it comes as no surprise, it is disturbing to confirm, again, that structural precarity is highly negatively correlated with physical health and psychological well-being, and positively correlated with suicidal ideation and involvement in trading sex for housing/services/goods. Turning to the evidence on discrimination, there is a parallel and unsurprising, pattern: Trans and nonbinary youth and youth of color experience significantly more everyday discrimination (people staring, misgendering, assuming incorrect gender, and being less respectful) than cisgender and White participants. These slights on the soul accumulate from adults in authority and from peers. Whether we ask about police, teachers, health care providers, religious leaders, bullying or cyber-bullying from peers, trans and nonbinary youth and youth of color report feeling far less respect than their cisgender and White peers.

Challenging Categories, Insisting on Complex Personhood, and Engaging in Activist Solidarities

While the patterns displayed above are as predictable as they are horrific, there are important surprises rising from this mass of surveys. Most young people challenge the very identity categories that social movements have historically relied upon; most tell very complex and layered stories about their identities and commitments, and for a significant core of LGBTQIA+ youth, the cumulative consequences of oppression provoke various forms of activism. In fact, our statistical analyses confirm that the more discrimination reported, the more activism and more varied forms of activism engaged—particularly by youth of color and trans/nonbinary respondents (i.e., scores on the everyday discrimination scale are significantly and positively associated with engagement in activism, correlations about .22, $p = .0000$).

Said simple, young people do not simply internalize rejection, betrayal, or social violence. Instead, they seem to draw strength while living in the borderlands, leaning on activist legacies, turning to social media, and joining with activist friends to challenge heteronormativity, gender binaries, poverty, and racism, and to suture solidarities among movements that have long been divided. Consider the comments (followed by demographic self-descriptions) elicited in response to two open-ended items from the survey: *"Tell us a story about your proudest moment."* and *"If you were to create a political banner, what would it say?"*

Across these prompts, young people are most proud in creativity and solitude, when they perform courageous acts of "being myself" and "letting others know who I am," as well as when they defend/support others.

"I was proudest of myself . . ."

When I was writing on my roof, alone. Watching the sun set, all the clouds changing trying to chase the day away, pulling the moon from the bliss of the horizon which at this moment was the hill sides coerced with dark evergreen trees scraping the sky. ("I'm a mutt," Native and White)

When I was 21 I came out to my parents and while it was definitely not my happiest moment, looking back now I would have to say it's my proudest. I had to work hard and overcome a lot of things internally to be who I am today. We were in a hotel room for my sister's volleyball tournament and I handed them a manila folder with a letter I had been writing for the past six months. Coming out to first generation immigrant Christian parents is not an easy feat. I broke their hearts when I told them who I was and while we are still in the process of figuring out how to love and understand each other, I'm glad I can die unapologetic about who I am or what I stand for. (lesbian, cis female, Chinese American)

When I graduated with my "male" color gown and my chosen name being called. All my family and school was there, and it reaffirmed everything I went through. I also felt proud because the majority of the people there didn't support me and I was throwing it in their faces. (trans man publicly, gender fluid, nonbinary personally, white)

When I came out to my friends as a sexual abuse survivor and spoke at a take-back-the-night event. (queer, cis-woman, White)

Others designed bold banners to explode narrow demographic categories and unveil their full and complex selves:

Queer, Trans, Asian, Disabled; Scientist, Artist, Actor. Imagine me complexly ("I have no idea anymore, really." Bigender, Japanese)

Transgender, nonbinary, autistic, proud (pansexual, demiboy, White)

Womyn, queer, immigrant, Mexican . . . How much more powerful could I get in this country? (Dykeness, cisgender, Mexican to the core, Maya/Aztec)

Recovering Catholic Republican, now queer and homeless. "And they'll know we are Christians by our love." (Bisexual, transman, Whiter than a Republican debate in the Alaska Panhandle)

Hug a Gay Mormon: We Exist!! (I am a boy who is attracted to other boys for emotional and physical reasons, I am Caucasian and my family stems from Europe . . . I am LDS but have Jewish heritage and practice both Jewish and Christian holidays, White)

Quite a few designed banners that confront those in power in order to posit a challenge to structural hierarchies, intersectionalities, and constraining binaries:

Just because I am a man with a vagina doesn't mean I can't be proud about it (gay, male, transman, Caucasian)

Flexing my complexion over White supremacy (Gay, boy, multiracial, Brazilian, Latino, Asian, Black)

Lesbians have more orgasms than straight women (Pansexual, primarily women, female, White but my father is mulatto and my grandparents were Black)

Speaking words of wisdom, let them pee (demisexual, a mess, man)

I was born gay, were you born an asshole? (natural, queer, woman, White)

How am I still here? (Blackity black, I'm black y'all and Afrolatinx)

We were all born naked and the rest is drag. (Goldstar, platinum, double mile day, male with some drag queer influences, sombrero AF, Latino, Native)

Don't judge a book by its genitals. (I like girls mostly but I'm not entirely comfortable with sex, most of the time I feel male but sometimes it's more blurry, I have constant bad feelings about my chest regardless, GNC, White)

Skin color is not probable cause (A queer, nonbinary, Black)

Finally, we hear young people who use the open-ended questions to stake out claims for intersectional activism and solidarities:

Vietnamese queer femme sorceress mermaid out to abolish the American state (queer, non-binary, gender non-conforming, genderqueer, Southeast Asian/Vietnamese)

Reparations for slavery and femme labor (queer, femme, Black)

Yellow Peril supports Black Power (lesbian, cis, biracial, Japanese/White)

> Disability is about a system of oppression, not about me being broken (straight, transman, White)

Even some relatively privileged youth sketched claims of their complexity, and obligation to justice, on their banners:

> Queer, Gender non-conforming and mixed race, these are a part of who I am and have pushed me to think critically and support those who have not been given the privileges I have taken for granted in the past (bisexual, queer, mixed race, Chicano/White)

Through queer lines of vision, these young people boldly announce their complexities and announce their solidarities.

THE OBLIGATIONS OF CRITICAL COMMUNITY INQUIRY

In a public lecture at Bergen Community College, writer Junot Diaz spoke to students about how vampires evolve, why we all need mirrors, and what happens when we don't see ourselves reflected:

> You know how vampires have no reflections in the mirror? If you want to make a human being a monster, deny them, at the cultural level, any reflection of themselves. . . . And growing up, I felt like a monster in some ways. I didn't see myself reflected at all. I was like, "Yo, is something wrong with me?" That the whole society seems to think that people like me don't exist? And part of what inspired me was this deep desire, that before I died, I would make a couple of mirrors. That I would make some mirrors, so that kids like me might see themselves reflected back and might not feel so monstrous for it. (Diaz, quoted by Stetler, 2009)

Like Diaz, as a research collective we take seriously our obligation to construct mirrors and design a wide range of WYI products—scholarly, online, blogs, videos, performance, amicus briefs, spoken word, poetry, comics—for a wide range of audiences, including families, teachers, youth, activists, legislators, and children about to awaken to gender, sexuality, and racial dynamics, desires, and ruptures. We are just beginning to collectively analyze the data, record videos, write poetry, produce instagrams, design T-shirts, and curate infographics . . . as we build an open access, on-line archive of the quantitative and qualitative material that will be available to activists, policymakers, and young people across the country.

In the belly of this archive is a rich appreciation for how much LGBTQ+/GNC young people embody and narrate the scars of oppression and at the same time speak in a dialect of "radical wit"; how much they experience betrayal and fraught relationships, and yet extend extraordinary generosity to peers and those younger. In response to structural exclusions and violence based on race, gender, disability, and/or sexuality, LGBTQ+/GNC youth seek three forms of justice:

- the right to be recognized for their full and complex selves *(justice of recognition)*;
- the disruption and transformation of economic, racial, gender, and sexual hierarchies *(justice of re-distribution)*, and
- deep involvement in shaping LGBTQ/GNC policy and research—"No Research on Us, Without Us" *(justice of participation)*.

In an interview, "Ask a Feminist: A conversation with Cathy Cohen on Black Lives Matter, feminism and activism" (2015), Cathy Cohen, Professor of political science at the University of Chicago, working with Chicago's Black Youth Project 100, referenced the long, buried legacy of Black queer women's radical social movement leadership in the United States:

> There have always been radical Black women or radical women engaged in mobilization, organizing, and leadership: we know that is not new. I do think what's new is the ways in which, at this moment in the Black Lives Matter movement, young Black often queer women are not just doing the work but are part of a collective leadership. The fact that they are visible and vocal, not just in one organization but across a number of organizations, shaping the direction of this movement—this is something that's new. And they are leading not specifically women's organizations but also what many of us recognize as Black liberation organizations. While the inclusion and in some cases leadership of women, queer, and LGBT folks in our movements is not new, these individuals, like Bayard Rustin, haven't always had the opportunity to be a visible or foreground part of the Black struggle. . . .

And then of course on July 27, 2017, the President tweeted that transgender soldiers would no longer be able to serve in the U.S. military, and the Attorney General asserted that sexual orientation should not be covered by the Civil Rights Act of 1964.

Echoes of exclusion and mobilizations for resistance swell, again. This too is U.S. history. But LGBTQ/GNC youth today, like others before and those coming after, braid criticism, dreams, and activism. Full-bodied, willful subjects, ready for the struggle.

"WILLFUL SUBJECTS"

In *Caliban and the Witch*, Silvia Federici (2014) chronicles the history of capitalist logic; she argues that revolting peasants, rebellious slaves, and undisciplined heretical witches had to be annihilated to prepare the grounds for capitalist logic and political economy. For capitalism to survive, Federici argues, the refusals of women and slaves had to be silenced; their transgressions had to be punished, shamed, and tamed. Rebellious slaves and women (and those who were both) were so dangerous that they had to be brutally erased.

One might ask who embodies *Caliban and the Witch* today? In the United States the current administration has targeted too many to name for annihilation, shaming, deportation, incarceration, institutionalization, and the denial of human rights. Here LGBTQ+/GNC youth (especially those of color) are indeed among the "witches" being hunted and mounted on the wall for display by a nation struggling to reclaim White supremacy, Christian fundamentalism, and heteronormativity, and to protect the very, very rich. At the moment, they are among the canaries in the neoliberal, White supremacist mine.

In their surveys, they report being targeted disproportionately in schools, on the streets, in subways, in airports, by public agencies and the police, and indeed often violated/betrayed at home. And yet perhaps more disturbing to those who would seek their annihilation, like *Caliban and the Witches*, they will not bow. Assimilation is not the goal. Acceptance and tolerance are not desired. Rather than pleading for inclusion, passing, remaining in the shadows, or allowing themselves to be silenced, LGBTQ/GNC youth stand tall as they seek recognition, demand redistribution, insist on participation, and embrace solidarities with Others under siege.

What's Your Issue was designed to provide a mirror, as Diaz hoped, and to chronicle the intersectional activist passions and commitments that Cohen recognized as a national (buried) treasure within LGBTQ+/ GNC communities of color. Our obligation has been, and continues to be, deeply shaped by and accountable to young people under siege. Together we decide how/when/to whom/for whom we provide open access to the data, for activists on the ground, for advocates involved in class action lawsuits, for policymakers gathering state testimony, for educators writing curriculum, for those youth in community organizations simply hoping not to become vampires, and for those leading social movements.

We end with their words:

My PGP (preferred gender pronoun) is PRISON ABOLITION (queer, GNC, butch, White)

I am #tamirrice I am #sandrabland I am #john crawford (straight?, nonbinary, two spirit, GNC, Peruvian)

I'm a borderline, hard of hearing, learning disabled genderfluid girl. GET OVER IT!

Critical Participatory Action Research and Knowledge Democracies

Lighting the Slow Fuse of the Research Imagination

> I use the term *wide-awakeness*. . . . Without the ability to think about yourself, to reflect on your life, there's really no awareness, no consciousness. Consciousness doesn't come automatically; it comes through being alive, awake, curious, and often furious.
>
> —Greene, 2008, p. 17

As you may remember from the opening of the book, I was born on the upward breeze of trans-national migration: My parents arrived as Jewish refugee children from Poland in the early 1920s—one an orphan and the other the 18th of 18 children from an orthodox Jewish family. I was born, the third of three, in the early 1950s in suburban New Jersey. My family was the (White) imaginary for mobility in the United States—the poster child story of meritocracy exploited to shame darker immigrants who came later. We were the story of "making it," an ideological fig leaf tossed over the racialized and classed oppressions festering at our national core. My upbringing did not destine me to be wide-awake to social injustice. Lulled by the anesthetic of Whiteness and post-war mobility, the rising status of my family, from plumbing supply beginnings, all seemed "natural."

As a preschooler I secured a front row seat to the EZ-pass of White suburban assimilation, class mobility, and the muffled contradictions of domestic heteronormativity. In 1950, (some) White fathers were a pastiche of testosterone, hard work, and the muscles of progress, while our mothers smelled like a cocktail of dinner and depression. Mine was a good life, not much scarring. I watched Jewish morph to

White, working class materialize to middle class as the plumbing supply truck was replaced by a Buick and a Christmas tree that arrived every year at the end of December.

A light, however, smuggled in through small fractures in our home on Summit Street, as James Baldwin (1964/2008) would later promise:

> One discovers the light in darkness, that is what darkness is for; but *everything in our lives depends on how we bear the light.* It is necessary, while in darkness, to know that there is a light somewhere, to know that in oneself, waiting to be found, there is a light. What the light reveals is danger, and what it demands is faith. . . . The light. The light. One will perish without the light. (p. 59, emphasis added)

The light nourished in me a healthy suspicion of narratives of progress, a desire to dig below narratives of despair, and the wisdom to know that the two were intimately entwined, in fact sleeping together. I came to mistrust any singular line of vision—even my own—and yearn for the wild possibilities that erupt when collectives gather, inquire, deconstruct the taken for granted, and re-imagine how else we might organize our social relations and institutions.

Maybe my mother's migraines saved me. A small dark spot on the white lung of cumulative mobility that propelled so many Jewish, Irish, Italian . . . immigrant families forward, moving so fast toward assimilation we could not pause to see or hear what was happening to Brown people, Spanish-speaking immigrants, Muslims, queers, White folks who didn't make it out of poverty, and those without documents. Maybe that's the debt of the baby daughter to notice, out of the corner of eyes otherwise glued to black-and-white TV, where *Father Knows Best* was blaring over frozen TV dinners, where even the dominant narrative would eventually tear. My little girl body longed perhaps for what French philosopher Paul Ricoeur (1970) would call "critical openness of suspicion and hope" (p. 27). But there are obligations of wide-awakeness to which we must now attend.

TO WHOM ARE WE ACCOUNTABLE?
PUBLIC SCIENCE AND NEOLIBERAL BLUES

Twenty years before she died, Maxine Greene—the stunning, brilliant existential philosopher, William F. Russell Professor of Foundations of Education at Teachers College, Columbia University, and Philosopher-in-Residence at the Lincoln Center Institute for the Arts in Education—delivered a lecture on the urgent need for radical imagination, and light. Haunted by the rise of neoliberalism and the yawning stretch of inequality gaps, Maxine watched the public schools she so loved lose funding and gain testing, lose the arts and gain police officers, lose life and gain standardization. To a rapt audience, she borrowed a line from poet Emily Dickinson to help push through the darkness:

> There are no promises, no guarantees. Emily Dickinson wrote that "The Possible's slow fuse is lit by the Imagination." It may at least be time to light the fuse. (Greene, 1994, p. 218)

Throughout her career, in her classrooms at Columbia and in salons in her living room, seasoning her lectures and embroidered in her writings, Maxine encouraged writers, teachers, researchers, and artists to reflect critically, engage full-bodily, and imagine boldly and collectively in times of despair. She insisted that we be open to "wide-awakenings" and refuse passivity. She implored us to invite our students to dream, organize, and conjure a more just tomorrow.

Privately, she of course had her anxieties, what she called her obsessions. We all did, and do. After most would exit the apartment on Fifth Avenue, a few of us would huddle up close at her dining room table or around her recliner chair, where she spoke of guilt and loss in her life, her privilege and the growing poverty just out her window, the swelling evidence of State and corporate betrayals of everyday people, the wonderful women who cared for her at the end of her life, the joyous protests that would march down Fifth Avenue as she would watch from above, and her deep disappointment with the dramatic disinvestment resulting in the erosion of public institutions, public life, and the collective good. She was dying at a moment in history when the lights of possibility were flickering. And yet on her deathbed in the hospital, she lifted her head and strained her voice to sing Solidarity Forever.

I take seriously my inheritance from activists and scholars I have known and loved: Linda Powell Pruitt, Thea Jackson, Maxine Greene, and Mort Deutsch speak to me often. They willed to us the obligation to gather and teach, analyze, study, and write alongside social movements and those who most intimately understand injustice; to design research collaboratively so we might imagine and mobilize for a different tomorrow; and never to trust our own solitary, privileged perspectives.

Like Maxine I worry—I know—that my line of vision has been obstructed by what critical race theorist and philosopher Charles Mills (2012) has called an *epistemology of ignorance*. For 30 years, as I've listened to school pushouts, women in prison, Muslim American youth, precariously housed LGBTQ youth, and the children of incarcerated parents, I am acutely aware of the joy of sitting with, but also the pain of what I never learned, *in my body*, about the very design of the United States. Pangs of hunger never consumed my belly, fear of police never shot through my nervous system, teachers never questioned my intellect, I always had a bed to call home, rejection was never inscribed in my family of origin, violence never touched my body. I know injustice well, but it's a closely held, cognitive acquaintance, an empathic muddle of solidarities, and a deep academic/political project. For those of us who have led relatively privileged lives, to be of use, as Marge Piercy would ask, we must be skeptical of the wisdom and limits of our own situated knowledges; we must begin with critical interrogation of how privilege shapes what we know and more so what we don't. And if we dare to venture into policy or research in "other people's communities," we must build knowledge, community, and public science with others, never in a comfortable, homogeneous gated community of self-appointed "experts."

PARTICIPATORY INQUIRY: BUILDING FRAGILE COMMUNITIES OF CRITICAL KNOWLEDGE AND ACTION

We are living, again and always, in contentious times. Many describe this as a moment of neoliberalism, and yet, sutured into the restructuring of the political economy, we witness a growing siege of State violence inflicted on the poor, working class, immigrants, LGBTQ youth, youth and communities of color; a vocal and vicious rise of White nationalism—we are at the mercy of a federal regime doubling down on deportations, police abuse, incarcerations, school closings; economic gifts to the wealthiest; denial of human(e) rights to those who struggle; and severe cuts in the social safety net. The question I seek to address, before we part, is what, if any, contribution toward justice might scholars, researchers, theorists, teachers, and writers offer? With whom, and toward what ends?

Given the troubling history of social science, one might reasonably conclude that science for the public good is oxymoronic; that research is inherently extractive and colonial, too easily bought and commodified; that universities are too elitist and soaked in a long history of exclusion, stratification, and White supremacy to be of use for generating counter-stories, gathering counter-evidence, or fueling movements for change.

And yet . . . in times of rising inequality and swelling precarity, neither despair nor retreat is acceptable. I want to insist that universities have an obligation to interrupt the social anesthesia; to provoke a wide-awakeness, to borrow from Maxine Greene; to awaken a sense of injustice, as argued by Morton Deutsch; to build what Robin Kelley (2017) calls "fugitive spaces" in the belly of the neoliberal academy; to do the work of subversion, contestation, and cultivation of what Jean Anyon called "radical possibilities" in research projects infused with critical dialogue, participatory analysis, debate, and dissent. Many have understandably given up on the academy as a space for liberatory work and view the university as a site in which critical dialogue is diluted; where academics/Whites/elites colonize or appropriate the ideas and suffering of Others, and get tenure. I understand. I have seen it. But still I yearn for, believe in, and commit to opening the public university to concerns of the common good, and to carving with others delicate spaces of collective criticality and public science where we interrogate privilege and argue through differences, forging what Audre Lorde called "meaningful coalitions" and designing research collectives drunk on a wide range of expertise and experience.

I do not want to overstate the influence or import of university teachers/researchers, or romanticize participatory research. Our withdrawal, however, evacuates a space that will be filled with anti-science ideologies and corporate-sponsored "science." And that blend is toxic.

It is important to consider how the ideologies and practices of injustice accelerate, and how researchers may be complicit, retreat, or accompany others in subverting the force and flow of such forces. History tells us that retreat and passivity breed complicity. We might look back to Hannah Arendt's writing on Eichmann in Jerusalem to discern how State, and corporate, violence gain traction and are reproduced through capillaries of compliance. After observing Eichmann's trial, Arendt (1963/2006) argued that evil is borne not primarily in active malevolence but in the slow non-thinking of the banal, in the everyday absence of critique, when passivity prevails and conformity is routinized. Twenty years later, in New Haven, Connecticut, Yale psychologist Irving Janis made an equally disturbing observation about the devastating consequences of false consensus embodied in and enacted by homogeneous workgroups of elites. Conformity and elitism produce distorted thinking, dangerous to Others, Janis concluded. In *GroupThink: Psychological Studies of Policy Decisions and Fiascoes* (1982), he sought to explain how intelligent policymakers—exquisitely educated White men—could lead the country into a series of what he called "policy fiascos" such as the Cuban Missile Crisis, the Vietnam War, and Watergate. Analyzing reams of archival documents and tapes, Janis argued that perverse, seriously flawed, and deadly decisions derive effortlessly from GroupThink—a collective consciousness that pervades when elite and homogeneous groups convene, seek consensus, assure one another of their moral superiority, eschew dissenting perspectives, and police group thought with "self-appointed mind guards—members who protect the group from adverse information that might shatter their shared complacency about the effectiveness and morality of their decisions" (pp. 174–175).

As political theorists and social psychological researchers, Arendt and Janis wrote on the dystopic conditions of uniformity and conformity that (re)produce evil and war. In those same years, however, educator-poet-activists Paulo Freire and Audre Lorde were sketching the radical possibilities unleashed by critical collective inquiry. In his classic volume *Pedagogy of the Oppressed*, Paulo Freire asserted critical inquiry as vital to humanity:

> For apart from inquiry, apart from the praxis, individuals can not be truly human. Knowledge emerges only through invention and re-invention, through the restless, impatient, continuing, hopeful inquiry human beings pursue in the world, with the world and with each other. (1970, p. 10)

A little more than a decade later, Audre Lorde also called for bold, critical, and collective inquiry and action. Referencing Freire, she warned against the urge, in dark times, to retreat into isolation, despair, or segregated spaces and insisted, instead, that people gather in "meaningful coalitions" to "find our work and do it."

> To refuse to participate in the shaping of our future is to give it up. Do not be misled into passivity either by false security (they don't mean me) or by despair (there's nothing we can do). Each of us must find our work and do it. Militancy no longer means guns at high noon, if it ever did. It means actively working for change, sometimes in the absence of any surety that change is coming. It means doing the unromantic and tedious work necessary to forge meaningful coalitions, and it means recognizing

which coalitions are possible and which coalitions are not. It means knowing that coalition, like unity, means the coming together of whole, self-actualized human beings, focused and believing, not fragmented automatons marching to a prescribed step. It means fighting despair. (Lorde, 1984, p. 240)

Laboring on different continents, embroiled in distinct movements for justice, Arendt and Janis understood compliance and GroupThink as dynamics that undermine democracy and our collective well-being, while Freire and Lorde understood deep collective inquiry to be vital for sustaining souls, building communities, and generating policies and movements for the common good.

Meanwhile, in South America, from the 1950s onward, academics and activists had been carving a long and embedded history of critical participatory action research in solidarity with liberation movements. In the campesinos de los Andres, coastal fishing villages, and with peasants in rural communities of Colombia, Orlando Fals Borda collaborated with land, labor, and cultural activists, mobilizing against state and social violence rooted in participatory action research and popular education. Along with Camilo Torres Restrepo and colleagues, these scholar-activists pursued a dual commitment to popular struggle and to transformation of the university. After producing a masterpiece volume with Eduardo Umaña Luna and Father German Guzman Campos, *La Violencia en Colombia* (Guzman Campos, Fals Borda, & Umaña Luna, 1962), detailing peasant slaughter in Colombia, Fals Borda came to believe that the obligation of the scholar was not simply to expose social realities but to try to transform unjust conditions, including the elitism of the academy. Along with his wife, Maria Cristina Salazar, Fals Borda contested the academic separation of thinking and feeling; the colonial privileging of academic knowledge; and the degradation of ethnic, indigenous, and Afro-descendent knowledges. They sought to open the university—what they called the plura-versity—to other logics, including ethnic, indigenous, and Afro-descendant epistemologies; they worked with communities to recover knowledges and construct within the university a subversive and ethical space for dialogue, collective memory, and reconciliation.

In April 1977 a small group of eminent Colombian social scientists met to convene the first World Symposium—Critica y Política en Ciencias Sociales—to interrogate history, politics, and social relations entrapped in the fight for land, in the farming crisis, and in the elite concentration of land ownership, made manifest in the struggles over drug wars, para-military assaults, and guerrilla violence. Alfredo Molano reflects on the 1977 gathering,

> As we sat there by the Caribbean, the Social Sciences were trying to break away from a Positivism without principle and at the same time become a critical . . . discipline. We started to take a new look, and a more critical and realistic one, at what was happening. This new way of looking at things, or rather perhaps of listening was what came to be called Participatory Action Research. . . . We were trying to show that personal commitment and political militancy for social change could themselves be serious scientific tasks. (1998, pp. 5, 7)

By 1995, Fals Borda railed against the elite monopoly on knowledge and sought instead collaborations with the "rebel, the heretic, the indigenous and common folk." Deeply ambivalent about whether the academy would be a worthy host to community-based research collectives, almost a quarter of a century ago Fals Borda admonished an audience of social researchers:

> Do not monopolise your knowledge nor impose arrogantly your techniques, but respect and combine your skills with the knowledge of the researched or grassroots communities, taking them as full partners and co-researchers. Do not trust elitist versions of history and science which respond to dominant interests, but be receptive to counter-narratives and try to recapture them. Do not depend solely on your culture to interpret facts but recover local values, traits, beliefs and arts for action by and with the research organisations. Do not impose your own ponderous scientific style for communicating results, but diffuse and share what you have learned together with the people, in a manner that is wholly understandable and every literary and pleasant, for science should not be necessarily a mystery nor a monopoly of experts and intellectuals. (1995)

As I write this book in the Summer of 2017, many of us from North America joined the 40th anniversary of that critical pilgrimage to Cartagena, Colombia, to reflect on and extend the legacy of critical research taken up by researchers, communities, and movements. Activist/community researchers and organizers from the Global South and North, from Peru, Brazil, India, South Africa, the United Kingdom, Australia, Canada, Ghana, New Zealand, Costa Rica, Colombia, Argentina, and refugees with no claim to a nation-state, gathered to bathe in the history—organizing local, cross-site, and cross-national possibilities for democratic knowledge production as a collective response to the multinational circuits of global capitalism and colonialism. Throughout the globe, and history, small groups of researchers—like independent journalists, including Du Bois after he left the academy—have worked with communities to unearth silenced histories and rebirth radical possibilities. And today, again, the need is great.

"PUBLIC" AT A CROSSROADS: BREAKING SILENCES, REVEALING RESISTANCE, AND PROVOKING POSSIBILITIES

At the 20th anniversary celebration of Democracy Now!, investigative reporter Juan Gonzalez reflected on the crucial role of independent broadcasting as a practice of bearing witness:

> We've been privileged to bear witness to the most important political events and social struggles of the past two decades, to interview some of the most brilliant grassroots leaders, artists, poets, scientists, from inmates bravely organizing within the prison-industrial complex to young immigrant DREAMers fighting to keep their families intact, to visionary political and religious leaders from around the world seeking to make a better life for their people, to American soldiers resisting imperial war from within the military, to daring whistleblowers exposing secrets, the darkest secrets of capitalism and empire. In the true spirit of the workingmen's press of the 1830s, the muckrakers of the early 1900s, the revolutionary press of the 1970s, we have sought to do our part to keep alive dissident alternative news and information and analysis, grounded in facts and research, and in the service of social progress. (Gonzalez, 2016)

In "Going to Where the Silence Is: Interview with Amy Goodman," we hear Goodman articulate the intimate relation of independent media and democracy; deeply respected for showing up on the front lines, at Standing Rock most recently, to interrogate and chronicle the questions, the struggles, the perspectives, and the resistance, Goodman offers:

> Independent media can go to where the silence is and break the sound barrier, doing what the corporate networks refuse to do. I think the media should be a sanctuary for dissent. That's what makes this country healthy. (McConnell, 2005)

Like independent and public media that feed and sustain democracy, it is important to acknowledge that all things public—public education and universities, public transportation, public arts and libraries, public land and parks, public sector trade unions, public housing and health care—are crucial to the soul of our collective well-being, even if deeply fraught. And they are ferociously under siege. In this context of resuscitating "public," I want to add public science as a collective practice for bearing witness, documenting injustice, revealing resistance, forging common interests, and provoking possibilities—a hybrid sanctuary for dissent, democracy, and social science.

If scholars and researchers are to be response-able to the aches of today, the banal and the grotesque, the injustice and the resistance, and join artists and writers, educators and students, organizers and policymakers in imagining a world not yet, Donna Haraway (2016) cautions that we must "stay with the trouble" (p. 1). In that spirit, critical PAR enjoys a proud, if suppressed, history of progressive critical inquiry, forged by citizen scientists, community and university researchers, artists, teachers, and activists, in the Global South and North, insisting on and enacting *No Research on Us Without Us* and thereby producing increasingly valid research.

Like those who came before, we present our evidence to international commissions (*We Charge Genocide*, 1951), perform our evidence in pageants (Du Bois, 2008/1911); integrate our analyses into courtrooms and litigation (Stoudt et al., 2015); challenge dominant narratives and circulate counter-stories in communities, organizations, movements, and theater (Fox & Fine, 2012); stitch forbidden lives onto embroideries (Segalo, 2016, 2015); produce counter-maps of occupied territories (Segalo, Manoff, & Fine, 2015); reveal wounds and resistance in videos (Cahill, Quijada Cerecer, & Bradley, 2010); invent new possibilities in sidewalk science, public art, spoken word, and popular education, and on T-shirts displaying quotes like "Why do I always fit the description?" (Stoudt et al., 2015); present evidence from the bottom-up in expert testimony, amicus briefs, scholarly articles, and brochures passed out at subway stations, in tweets, Instagrams, and Snapchats (see Lykes & Coquillon, 2009), and also in books, journals, chapters, and articles.

And so I leave you, 200 days into the Trump administration—when public lands, public media, public universities and schools, public transportation and infrastructure, civil rights, voting rights, reproductive rights, queer rights, the flows of immigration, public health care, and clean air and clean water are threatened; when police brutality, international conflict, privatization of public education, dismantling of the commons, tax breaks for the rich, and deportation and incarceration constitute the national agenda. I ask that you recall the words of Antonio Gramsci—almost 90 years ago—about surviving crisis. When morbid symptoms saturate the everyday, and bodies are falling and dreams curdling in our midst, when public life, institutions, and human rights are shattered in plain sight, social scientists have an obligation to bear witness, forge solidarities, craft collective inquiry, and produce documents for and with communities and policy, for theory and organizing, for teaching in the university and on the streets.

I hope I leave you moved by the rich vibrancies of participatory action research erupting across the globe and throughout history; the urgency and joy of trans-national collective inquiry rising from scars and wisdom, trauma and science, dissent and solidarity, statistics and stories, resistance and imagination. Like the arts, independent media, and social movements, in moments of crisis, critical participatory action research can carve open delicate spaces for fragile solidarities and collective inquiries, and even more valid research, where we might join with others to collectively ignite the slow fuse of the possible.

References

Abu El-Haj, T. (2015) *Unsettled belonging: Educating Palestinian American youth after 9/11*. Chicago, IL: University of Chicago Press.

Ahmed, S. (2014). *Willful subjects*. Durham, NC: Duke University Press.

Anand, B., Fine, M., Perkins, T., Surrey, D., & the Renaissance Graduating Class of 2000. (2002). *Keeping the struggle alive*. New York, NY: Teachers College Press.

Anyon, J. (2005). *Radical possibilities: Public policy, urban education and a new social movement*. New York, NY: Routledge.

Anzaldúa, G. (1987). *Borderlands/La frontera: The new Mestiza*. San Francisco, CA: Aunt Lute.

Appadurai, A. (2006). The right to research. *Globalisation, Societies and Education, 4*(2), 167–177. doi: 10.1080/14767720600750696

Arendt, H. (2006). *Eichmann in Jerusalem: The banality of evil report*. New York, NY: Penguin Books. (Original work published 1963)

Arshad, A. (2016). Citizens under suspicion: Responsive research with community under surveillance. *Anthropology & Education Quarterly, 47*, 78–95.

Ayala, J. (2006). Confianza, consejos, and contradictions: Gender and sexuality lessons between Latina adolescent daughters and mothers. In J. Denner & B. L. Guzmán (Eds.), *Latina girls: Voices of adolescent strength in the United States* (pp. 29–43). New York, NY: New York University Press.

Ayers, R., Ayers, W., Dohrn, B., & Jackson, T. (2001) *Zero tolerance*. New York, NY: The New Press.

Baldwin, J. (2008). Nothing personal. *Contributions in Black Studies, 6*(1), Article 5. Retrieved from scholarworks.umass.edu/cibs/vol6/iss1/5

Berlant, L. (2007). Slow death (sovereignty, obesity, lateral agency). *Critical Inquiry, 33*(4), 754–780.

Bhatia, S. (2007). *American karma: Race, culture, and identity in the Indian diaspora*. New York, NY: New York University Press.

Boal, A. (1979). *The theatre of the oppressed*. New York, NY: Urizen Books.

Bowen, W., & Bok, D. (1998). *The shape of the river*. Princeton, NJ: Princeton University Press.

Bowles, S., & Gintis, H. (1976). *Schooling in capitalist America: Educational reform and the contradictions of economic life*. New York, NY: Routledge.

Brodkin, K. (1998). *How Jews became white folks and what that says about race in America*. New Brunswick, NJ: Rutgers University Press.

124

Bryk, A. S., & Schneider, B. (2003). Trust in schools: A core resource for school reform. *Educational Leadership, 60*(6), 40–45.

Cahill, C., Quijada Cerecer, D. A., & Bradley, M. (2010). "Dreaming of . . .": Reflections on participatory action research as a feminist praxis of critical hope. *Affilia, 25*(4), 406–416.

Cammarota, J., & Fine, M. (2008). *Revolutionizing education: Youth PAR in motion.* New York, NY: Routledge.

Center for the Study of Hate and Extremism. (2016). *Arabs and Muslims saw more increases in bias-related crime than any other group.* San Bernardino, CA: Center for the Study of Hate and Extremism.

Cesaire, A. (1990). *Lyric and dramatic poetry, 1946–1982.* Charlottesville, VA: University of Virginia Press.

Cetina, K. K. (1999). *Epistemic cultures: How the sciences make knowledge.* Cambridge, MA: Harvard University Press.

Chajet, L. (2007). The power and limits of small schools. In D. Carlson (Ed.), *Keeping the promise: Essays on leadership, democracy, and education* (pp. 287–302). New York, NY: Peter Lang.

Christensen, C. (2015). Disruptive innovation. Retrieved from claytonchristensen.com/key-concepts/

Cohen, C., & Jackson, S. (2015). Ask a feminist: A conversation with Cathy Cohen on Black Lives Matter, feminism, and contemporary activism. Retrieved from signsjournal.org/ask-a-feminist-cohen-jackson

Collins, P. H. (1998). *Fighting words: Black women and the search for justice.* Minneapolis, MN: University of Minnesota Press.

Cooke, B., & Kothari, U. (2001). *Participation: The new tyranny?* London, England: Zed.

Correctional Association of New York. (2007, November 1). Protecting the rights of incarcerated parents and children. Retrieved from correctionalassociation.org/news/protecting-the-rights-of-incarcerated-parents-and-their-children

Cottom, T. M. (2012, December 9). Risks and ethics in public scholarship. Retrieved from insidehighered.com/blogs/university-venus/risk-and-ethics-public-scholarship

Crenshaw, K. (1995). Mapping the margins: Intersectionality, identity politics, and violence against women of colour. In K. Crenshaw, N. Gotanda, G. Peller, & K. Thomas (Eds.), *Critical race theory: The key writings that formed the movement* (pp. 357–383). New York, NY: New Press.

Cross, W. E., Jr. (1991). *Shades of Black.* Philadelphia, PA: Temple University Press.

Cross, W. E., Jr. (2003). Tracing the historical origins of youth delinquency and violence: Myth and reality about Black culture. *Journal of Social Issues, 59*, 67–82.

Darling-Hammond, L. (2010). *The flat world and education.* New York, NY: Teachers College Press.

Davis, A. (2003). *Are prisons obsolete?* New York, NY: Seven Stories Press.

De la Torre, M., & Gwynne, J. (2009). *When schools close: Effects on displaced students in Chicago public schools*. Chicago, IL: Consortium on Chicago School Research at the University of Chicago Urban Education Institute.

de Sousa Santos, B. (2014). *Epistemologies of the South: Justice against epistemicide*. New York, NY: Routledge.

Delpit, L. (1993). The silenced dialogue: Power and pedagogy in educating other people's children. In L. Weis & M. Fine (Eds.), *Beyond silenced voices* (pp. 119–142). Albany, NY: State University of New York Press. See also *Harvard Educational Review, 58*(3), August, 1988.

Diamond, L. (2009). *Sexual fluidity: Understanding women's love and desire*. Cambridge, MA: Harvard University Press.

Du Bois, W. E. B. (1899). *The Philadelphia negro: A social study*. Philadelphia, PA: Ginn.

Du Bois, W. E. B. (1903, November). *The Crisis Magazine, 6*, 339–345.

Du Bois, W. E. B. (1904). *The souls of black folk*. Chicago, IL: A. C. McClurg & Co.

Du Bois, W. E. B. (2008). *The quest of the silver fleece*. New York, NY: Dover Publishers. (Original work published 1911)

Durán-Narucki, V. (2008). School building condition, school attendance, and academic achievement in New York City public schools: A mediation model. *Journal of Environmental Psychology, 28*, 278–286.

Eccles, J. S., & Roeser, R. W. (2011). Schools as developmental contexts during adolescence. *Journal of Research on Adolescence, 21*(1), 225–241.

Evans, G. (2004, February/March). Environments of childhood poverty. *American Psychologist, 59*(2), 77–92.

Fabricant, M., & Fine, M. (2012). *Charter schools and the corporate makeover of public education*. New York, NY: Teachers College Press.

Fabricant, M., & Fine, M. (2013). *The changing politics of education: Privatization and the dispossessed lives left behind*. New York, NY: Paradigm.

Fals Borda, O. (1995). Research for social justice: Some north-south convergences. Keynote at the Southern Sociological Society, University of Tennessee. Retrieved from comm-org.wisc.edu/si/falsborda.html

Fanon, F. (1967). *Black skin, white masks*. New York, NY: Grove Press.

Federici, S. (2014). *Caliban and the witch*. Brooklyn, NY: Autonomedia.

Fine, M. (1988). Sexuality, schooling, and adolescent females: The missing discourse of desire. *Harvard Educational Review, 58*(1), 29–51.

Fine, M. (1991). *Framing dropouts: Notes on the politics of an urban public high school*. Albany, NY: State University of New York Press.

Fine, M. (1994). Working the hyphens: Reinventing the self and other in qualitative research. In N. Denzin & Y. Lincoln (Eds.), *Handbook of qualitative research* (pp. 70–82). Newbury Park, CA: Sage.

Fine, M. (2006, March). Bearing witness—Methods for researching oppression and resistance: A textbook for critical research methods. *Social Justice Research, 19*(1), 83–108.

Fine, M. (2012). Troubling calls for evidence: A critical race, class and gender analysis of whose evidence counts. *Feminism and Psychology, 22,* 3–19.

Fine, M., & Barreras, R. (2001). To be of use. *Analyses of Social Issues and Public Policy.* Retrieved from onlinelibrary.wiley.com/doi/10.1111/1530-2415. 00012/epdf

Fine, M., Bloom, J., Burns, A., Chajet, L., Guishard, M., Payne, Y., & Torre, M. E. (2005). Dear Zora: A letter to Zora Neal Hurston fifty years after *Brown. Teachers College Record, 107*(3), 496–528.

Fine, M., & Burns, A. (2003, December). Class notes: Toward a critical psychology of class and schooling. *Journal of Social Issues, 59*(4), 841–860.

Fine, M., Burns, A., Payne, Y., & Torre, M. E. (2004). Civics lessons: The color and class of betrayal. *Teachers College Record, 106,* 2193–2223.

Fine, M., Roberts, R., Torre, M. E., Bloom, J., Burns, A., Chajet, L., . . . Payne, Y. (2004). *Echoes of Brown: Youth documenting and performing the legacy of Brown v. Board of Education.* New York, NY: Teachers College Press.

Fine, M., & Ruglis, J. (2009). Circuits and consequences of dispossession: The racialized realignment of the public sphere for U.S. youth. *Transforming Anthropology, 17*(1), 20–33.

Fine, M., & Torre, M. E. (2004). Re-membering exclusions: Participatory action research in public institutions. *Qualitative Research in Psychology 1*(1), 15–37.

Fine, M., Torre, M. E., Boudin, K., Bowen, I., Clark, J., Hylton, D., . . . Upegui, D. (2003). Participatory action research: Within and beyond bars. In P. Camic, J. E. Rhodes, & L. Yardley (Eds.), *Qualitative research in psychology: Expanding perspectives in methodology and design* (pp. 173–198). Washington, DC: American Psychological Association.

Fine, M., Tuck, J. E., & Zeller-Berkman, S. (2007). Do you believe in Geneva? In N. Denzin, L. T. Smith, & Y. Lincoln (Eds.), *Handbook of critical and indigenous knowledges* (pp. 157–180). Beverley Hills, CA: Sage.

Fine, M., Weis, L., Pruitt, L. P., & Burns, A. (2004). *Off white: Readings of power, privilege and resistance.* New York, NY: Routledge.

Fine, M., Weis, L., Wong, L. M., & Weseen, S. (2000). For whom? Qualitative research, representations, and social responsibilities. In N. Denzin & Y. Lincoln (Eds.), *The handbook of qualitative research* (2nd ed., pp. 107–131). Thousand Oaks, CA: Sage.

Foucault, M. (1977). *Discipline and punish: The birth of the prison.* New York, NY: Pantheon.

Fox, M., & Fine, M. (2012). Circulating critical research: Reflections on performance and moving inquiry into action. In G. Cannella & S. Steinberg (Eds.), *Critical qualitative research reader* (pp. 153–165). New York, NY: Peter Lang.

Fraser, N. (1995). Recognition or redistribution? A critical reading of Iris Young. *Journal of Political Philosophy, 32,* 166–180.

Freire, P. (1970). *Pedagogy of the oppressed.* New York, NY: Herder and Herder.

Fullilove, M. (2009). *Root shock: How tearing up city neighborhoods hurts America, and what we can do about it.* Random House Digital, Inc.

Futch, V., & Fine, M. (2014). Mapping as a method: History and theoretical commitments. *Qualitative Research in Psychology, 22*(1), 42–59.

Galletta, A. (2012). *Declaration on the impact of school closure in south Sacramento.* Cleveland, OH: Cleveland State University.

Gangi, R., Schiraldi, V., & Ziedenberg, J. (1998). *New York state of mind? Prison vs. higher education funding in the empire state.* New York, NY: Correctional Association of New York.

Gaventa, J. (1980). *Power and powerlessness: Quiescence and rebellion in an Appalachian valley.* Chicago, IL: University of Illinois Press.

Goffman, E. (1959). *The presentation of self in everyday life.* New York, NY: Doubleday.

Gonzalez, J. (2016, December 6). Juan González on 20 years of Democracy Now! & keeping dissident alternative news alive. Retrieved from democracynow.org/2016/12/6/juan_gonzalez_on_20_years_of

Gordon, A. (1997). *Ghostly matters: Haunting and the sociological imagination.* Minneapolis, MN: University of Minnesota Press.

Gramsci, A. (1971). *Selections from prison notebooks.* New York, NY: International Publishers.

Greene, M. (n.d.). Imagination and becoming. Retrieved from maxinegreene.org/uploads/library/imagination_bbcs.pdf

Greene, M. (1977). Toward wide-awakeness: An argument for the arts and humanities in education. *Teachers College Record, 79*(1), 119–125.

Greene, M. (1994). Postmodernism and the crisis of representation. *English Education, 26,* 206–219.

Greene, M. (2008). Education and art: Windows of imagination. *Learning Landscapes, 1,* 17–21.

Greenhaven Think Tank. (1997). *The non-traditional approach to criminal and social justice.* New York, NY: Center for NuLeadership, Resurrection Study Group.

Guzman Campos, G., Fals Borda, O., & Umaña Luna, E. (1962). *La violencia en Colombia: Estudio de un proceso social* (2nd ed.). Colombia: Ediciones Tercer Mundo.

Haraway, D. (2016). *Staying with the trouble.* Durham, NC: Duke University Press.

Harding, S. (1994). Rethinking standpoint epistemology: What is "strong objectivity"? In L. Alcoff & E. Potter (Eds.), *Feminist epistemologies* (pp. 49–82). New York, NY: Routledge.

Harney, S., & Moten, F. (2013). The undercommons: Fugitive planning & black study. Retrieved from minorcompositions.info/wp-content/uploads/2013/04/undercommons-web.pdf

Harris, C. (1993). Whiteness as property. *Harvard Law Review, 8,* 1710–1794.

Harvey, D. (2003). *The new imperialism.* Oxford, England: Oxford University Press.

Hernandez, J. (2009, February 3). Giant Manhattan school to be broken up to further smaller-is-better policy. *New York Times,* A27. Retrieved from nytimes.com/2009/02/04/education/04brandeis.html hooks, b. (1989). Choosing the margin as a space of radical openness. In b. hooks (Ed.), *Yearning: Race, gender and cultural politics* (pp. 203–209). Boston, MA: South End Press.

Jahoda, M., Lazarsfeld, P., & Zeisel, H. (2001). *Marienthal: The sociography of an unemployed community.* London, England: Transaction Publications.

Janis, I. (1982). *GroupThink: Psychological studies of policy decisions and fiascoes* (2nd ed.). Boston, MA: Wadsworth/Cengage.

Janoff-Bulman, R. (2010). *Shattered assumptions.* New York, NY: Simon and Schuster.

Journey for Justice Alliance. (2013). *Death by a thousand cuts.* Chicago, IL: Author. Retrieved from j4jalliance.com/wp-content/uploads/2014/02/J4JReport-final_05_12_14.pdf

Katz, C. (2001). On the grounds of globalization: A topography for feminist political engagement. *Signs, 26*(4), 1213–1234.

Katz, C. (2003). *Growing up global.* Minneapolis, MN: University of Minnesota Press.

Kelley, R. D. G. (2003). *Freedom dreams: The Black radical imagination.* Boston, MA: Beacon.

Kelley, R. D. G. (2017). Black study, black struggle. Retrieved from bostonreview.net/forum/robin-d-g-kelley-black-study-black-struggle

King, J. (2015). *Dysconscious racism, Afrocentric praxis and education for liberation.* New York, NY: Routledge.

King, J., & Swartz, E. (2014). *Re-membering history in student and teacher learning: An Afrocentric culturally informed praxis.* New York, NY: Routledge.

Kliewer, W., & Lepore, S. J. (2015). Exposure to violence, social cognitive processing, and sleep problems in urban adolescents. *Journal of Youth and Adolescence, 8*(3), 427–436.

Krenichyn, K., Saegert, S., & Evans, G. (2001). Parents as moderators of psychological and physiological correlates of inner city children's exposure to violence. *Applied Developmental Psychology, 22,* 581–602.

Ladson-Billings, G. (2006). Presidential address: From the achievement gap to the education debt: Understanding achievement in U.S. schools. *Educational Researcher, 35*(7), 3–12.

Ladson-Billings, G. (2011). Boyz to men? Teaching to restore Black boys' childhood. *Race, Ethnicity and Education, 14*(1), 7–15.

Latour, B. (2004, Winter). Why has critique run out of steam? From matters of fact to matter of concern. *Critical Inquiry, 30,* 225–248.

Latour, B., & Woolgar, S. (1979). *Laboratory life: The construction of scientific facts.* Beverly Hills, CA: Sage.

Lewis, M. (1992). *Shame and the exposed self.* New York, NY: Free Press.

Lipman, P. (2011). *The new political economy of urban education.* New York, NY: Routledge.

Lorde, A. (1984). *Sister outsider: Essays and speeches.* Trumansburg, NY: The Crossing Press.

Lorey, I. (2015). *State of insecurity.* London, England: Verso.

Luttrell, W. (2013). Children's counter-narrative of care: Towards educational justice. *Children and Society, 27,* 195–308.

Luxembourg, R. (2003). *Accumulation of capital.* New York, NY: Routledge. (Original work published 1913)

Lykes, M. B. (2012). One legacy among many: The Ignacio Martín-Baró Fund for Mental Health and Human Rights at 21. *Peace and Conflict: Journal of Peace Psychology, 18*(1), 88–95.

Lykes, M. B., & Coquillon, E. D. (2009). Psychosocial trauma, poverty, and human rights in communities emerging from war. In D. Fox, I. Prilleltensky, & S. Austin (Eds.), *Critical psychology* (vol. II, pp. 285–299). London, England: Sage.

Lykes, M. B., & Moane, G. (2009). Whither feminist liberation psychology? Critical exploration of feminist and liberation psychologies for a globalizing world. *Feminism & Psychology, 19*(3), 283–298.

Maira, S. (2004). Youth culture, citizenship and globalization: South Asian Muslim youth in the United States after September 11th. *Comparative Studies of South Asia, Africa and the Middle East, 24*(1), 219–231.

Maldonado-Torres, N. (2007, March/May). On the coloniality of being. *Cultural Studies, 21*(2), 240–270.

Marquez-Lewis, C., Fine, M., Boudin, K., Waters, W., DeVeaux, M., Vargas, F., Wilkins, C., Martinez, M., Pass, M., & White-Harrigan, S. (2013, December). How much punishment is enough? Designing participatory research on parole policies for persons convicted of violent crimes. *Journal of Social Issues, 69*(4), 771–796.

Martin, E. (2016). The ethnography of experimental psychology. Lecture in Critical Psychology program, The Graduate Center, CUNY.

Martín-Baró, I. (1990, March 23). Reparations: Attention must be paid. *Commonweal,* 184–186.

Martín-Baró, I. (1994). *Writings for a liberation psychology.* Cambridge, MA: Harvard University Press.

Massey, S., & Barreras, R. (2013). Impact validity as a framework for advocacy based research. *Journal of Social Issues, 69*(4), 615–632.

McConnell, C. (2005, February 2). Going to where the silence is: Interview with Amy Goodman. Retrieved from yesmagazine.org/issues/media-that-set-us-free/going-to-where-the-silence-is-interview-with-amy-goodman

McCord, R. (2002). Declaration of Dr. Robert S. McCord in *San Francisco NAACP et al. vs. San Francisco Unified School District.*

McEwen, B. (2000). Allostasis and allostatic load. *Neuropsychopharmacology, 22,* 108–124.

McEwen, B. (2012). Brain on stress: How the social environment gets under the skin. *Proceedings of the National Academy of Sciences of the United States of America, 10–16*(109), 17180–17185.

McKittrick, K. (2006). *Demonic grounds: Black women and the cartographies of struggle.* Minneapolis, MN: University of Minnesota Press.

Melamed, J. (2011). *Represent and destroy*. Minneapolis, MN: University of Minnesota Press.

Milgram, S., & Jodelet, D. (1976). Psychological maps of Paris. In H. M. Proshansky, et al. (Eds.), *Environmental psychology: People and their physical settings* (2nd ed., pp. 104–125). New York, NY: Holt, Rinehart and Winston.

Mills, C. (2012). White ignorance. In S. Sullivan & N. Tuana (Eds.), *Race and epistemologies of ignorance* (pp. 13–38). Albany, NY: State University of New York Press.

Molano, A. (1998). Cartagena revisited twenty years on. In O. Fals Borda (Ed.), *People's participation: Challenges ahead* (pp. 3–10). Bogota: Colombia: Conciencias, IEPRi, TM Editores.

Morawski, J. (1997). The science behind feminist research methods. *The Journal of Social Issues, 53*(4), 667–681.

Muñoz-Proto, C., Lyon, A. D., Castillo, C. V., & Battistella, M. (2013, December). Memoscopio: Producing usable and collectively owned knowledge about the World March for Peace and Nonviolence. *Journal of Social Issues, 69*(4), 754–770.

Nakamura, J., & Csikszentmihalyi, M. (2002). The concept of flow. In C. R. Snyder & S J. Lopez (Eds.), *Handbook of positive psychology* (pp. 89–105). Oxford, England: Oxford University Press.

Noguera, P. (2003). *City schools and the American dream*. New York, NY: Teachers College Press.

Oakes, J. (1988, January). Tracking: Can schools take a different route? *NEA Today, 6*(6), 41–47.

Olsen, T. (1984). *Mother to daughter/Daughter to mother*. London, England: Virago.

Painter, N. (1995). Soul murder and slavery: Toward a fully-loaded cost accounting. In L. K. Kerber, A. Kessler-Harris, & K. K. Sklar (Eds.), *U.S. history as women's history: New feminist essays* (pp. 125–146). Chapel Hill, NC: University of North Carolina Press.

Patel, L. (2016). *Decolonizing educational research: From ownership to answerability*. New York, NY: Routledge.

Payne, Y., & Brown, T. (2016). "I'm still waiting on the golden ticket." *Journal of Social Issues, 72*(4), 789–811.

People's Knowledge Editorial Collective. (2016). *People's knowledge and participatory action research: Escaping the white walled labyrinth*. Rugby, UK: Practical Action Publications.

Pratt, M. L. (1991). Arts of the contact zone. *Profession, 33*–40. Retrieved from fiu.edu/~ereserve/010035191-1.pdf

Pruitt, L. P. (2004). The achievement (k)not. In M. Fine, L. Weis, L. P. Pruitt, & A. Burns (Eds.), *Off white: Readings on power, privilege, and resistance* (pp. 235–244). New York, NY: Routledge.

Pruitt, L. P. (2011). *Changing minds, changing schools*. Richmond, VA: Leaven Press. (Original work published 2000)

Puar, J. (2012). Precarity talk: A virtual roundtable with Lauren Berlant, Judith Butler, Bojana Cvejiç, Isabell Lorey, Jasbir Puar, and Ana Vujanoviç. *TDR/The Drama Review, 56*(4), 163–177.

Rabaka, R. (2010). *Against epistemic apartheid: W. E. B. Du Bois and the disciplinary decadence of sociology*. Lexington, MA: Lexington Books.

Reardon, J., Metcalf, J., Kenney, M., & Barad, K. (2015). Science & justice: The trouble and the promise. *Catalyst: Feminism, Theory, and Technoscience, 1*(1), 1–48.

Rethinking Schools. (2005). Small schools, big issues. *Rethinking Schools, 19*(4).

Ricoeur, P. (1970). *Freud and philosophy: An essay on interpretation*. New Haven, CT: Yale University Press.

Rittel, H., & Webber, M. (1973). Dilemmas in a general theory of planning. *Policy Sciences, 4*, 155–169.

Robinson, C. (1993). *Black Marxism*. Chapel Hill, NC: University of North Carolina.

Rogers, J., & Mirra, N. (2014). It's about time. Los Angeles, CA: IDEA, UCLA. Retrieved from idea.gseis.ucla.edu/projects/its-about-time

Rogowski, J., & Cohen, C. (2015, October). *Black Youth Project millennials report*. Chicago, IL: Center for the Study of Race, Politics and Culture, University of Chicago.

Roy, A. (2003, January 27). Confronting empire. Retrieved from ratical.org/ratville/CAH/AR012703.html

Saegert, S., & Winkel, G. (1999, March 1). CDC, social capital and housing. *Shelterforce*. Washington DC: National Housing Institute. Retrieved from shelterforce.org/1999/03/01/cdcs-social-capital-and-housing-quality/

Said, E. (2012). *On lost causes: Reflections on exile and other essays*. London, England: Granta.

Sandwick, T., Fine, M., Stoudt, B., Torre, M. E., Greene, A. C. & Patel, L. (forthcoming). Promise & provocation: Humble reflections on critical participatory action research for social policy. *Urban Education*.

Schott Foundation. (2013). The color of school closures. Retrieved from schottfoundation.org/blog/2013/04/05/color-school-closures

Scott, J. (1990). *Domination and the arts of resistance: Hidden transcripts*. New Haven, CT: Yale University Press.

Segalo, P. (2012, August). Gendered suffering and the complexities of keeping silent. *Studia Historiae Ecclesiasticae, XXXVIII* (Supplement), 113–122.

Segalo, P. (2013, November). Women, they too have their story: Re-imagining the female voice and body. *Scriptura, 112*, 1–10.

Segalo, P. (2014). Embroidery as narrative: Black South African women's experiences of suffering and healing. *Agenda, 28*(1), 44–53.

Segalo, P. (2015). Trauma and gender. *Social and Personality Psychology Compass, 9*(9), 447–454.

Segalo, P. (2016). Using cotton, needles and threads to break the women's silence: Embroideries as a decolonising framework. *Journal of Inclusive Education, 20*(3), 246–260.

Segalo, P., Manoff, E., & Fine, M. (2015). Working with embroideries and counter-maps: Engaging memory and imagination within decolonizing frameworks. *Journal of Social and Political Psychology, 3*(1), 342–364.

Sennett, J., & Cobb, R. (1993). *The hidden injuries of class.* New York, NY: Norton.

Sirin, S. R., & Fine, M. (2007). Hyphenated selves: Muslim American youth negotiating identities on the fault lines of global conflict. *Applied Developmental Science, 11*(3), 1–13.

Sirin, S. R., & Fine, M. (2008). *Muslim American youth: Understanding hyphenated identities through multiple methods.* New York, NY: New York University Press.

Smith, L. T. (1999). *Decolonizing methodologies: Research and indigenous peoples.* London, England: Zed Books.

Smith, L. T. (2005). On tricky grounds: Researching the native in an age of uncertainty. In N. Denzin & Y. Lincoln (Eds.), *Handbook of qualitative research* (pp. 85–107). Beverly Hills, CA: Sage.

Sojoyner, D. (2016). *First strike: Educational enclosures in Black Los Angeles.* Minneapolis, MN: University of Minnesota Press.

Spivak, G. (1988). Can the subaltern speak? In C. Nelson & L. Grossberg (Eds.), *Marxism and the interpretation of culture* (pp. 271–313). Chicago, IL: University of Illinois Press.

Stetler, C. (2009, October 26). Junot Diaz: Man in the mirror. Retrieved from nj.com/entertainment/arts/index.ssf/2009/10/junot_diaz_man_in_the_mirror.html

Stevens, G., Duncan, N., & Hook, D. (2013). *Race, memory and the Apartheid archives.* London, England: Palgrave MacMillan.

Stoudt, B., Fine, M., & Fox, M. (2011/2012). Growing up policed in the age of aggressive policing policies. *New York Law School Law Review, 56,* p. 4.

Stoudt, B. G., & Torre, M. E. (2014). The Morris Justice Project. Retrieved from methods.sagepub.com/case/the-morris-justice-project-participatory-action-research

Stoudt, B. G., Torre, M. E., Bartley, P., Bracy, F., Caldwell, H., Downs, A., Greene, C., Haldipur, J., Hassan, P., Manoff, E., Sheppard, N., & Yates, J. (2015). "We come from a place of knowing": Experiences, challenges, advantages and possibilities of participating in Morris Justice Project. In C. Durose & L. Richardson (Eds.), *Re-thinking public policy making: Why co-production matters* (pp. 125–137). Bristol, England: Policy Press.

Sullivan, S., & Tuana, N. (2007). *Race and the epistemologies of ignorance.* Albany, NY: State University of New York Press.

Teo, T. (2010). What is epistemological violence in the social sciences? *Social and Personality Psychology Compass, 4*(5), 295–303.

Torre, M. E. (2009). Participatory action research and critical race theory: Fueling spaces for nosotras to research. *The Urban Review, 41*(1), 106–120.

Torre, M. E., & Ayala, J. (2009). Envisioning participatory action research entremundos. *Feminism and Psychology, 19*(3), 387–393.

Torre, M. E., Fine, M., Stoudt, B., & Fox, M. (2012). Critical participatory action research as public science. In P. Camic & H. Cooper (Eds.), *The handbook of qualitative research in psychology: Expanding perspectives in methodology and design* (2nd ed., pp. 171–184). Washington, DC: American Psychological Association.

U.S. Department of Education. (2016). Fast facts. Closed schools [National Center for Educational Statistics]. Retrieved from nces.ed.gov/fastfacts/display.asp?id=619

United States Interagency Council on Homelessness. (2015, November). Fiscal Year 2015 Performance and Accountability Report. Retrieved from usich.gov/resources/uploads/asset_library/FY2015-USICH-PAR.pdf

Valenzuela, A. (1999). *Subtractive schooling*. Albany, NY: State University of New York Press.

Velasquez-Manoff, M. (2013, July 27). Status and stress. Retrieved from opinionator.blogs.nytimes.com/2013/07/27/status-and-stress/

Vizenor, G. R. (1994). *Manifest manners: Postindian warriors of survivance*. Middletown, CT: Wesleyan University Press.

Vizenor, G. R. (2008). *Survivance: Narratives of native presence*. Lincoln, NE: University of Nebraska Press.

We Charge Genocide. (1951). Retrieved from blackpast.org/we-charge-genocide-historic-petition-united-nations-relief-crime-united-states-government-against

Weis, L., & Fine, M. (2012, Summer). Critical bifocality and circuits of privilege. *Harvard Educational Review, 82*(2), 173–201.

Werner, C., & Altman, I. (1998). A dialectical/transactional framework of social relations. In D. Gorlitz (Ed.), *Children, cities and psychological theories* (pp. 123–150). Berlin, Germany: Walter de Gruytur Publishers.

Wike, R. (2016). What the world thinks about climate change in 7 charts. Retrieved from pewresearch.org/fact-tank/2016/04/18/what-the-world-thinks-about-climate-change-in-7-charts/

Willis, P. (1977). *Learning to labour: How working class kids get working class jobs*. Aldershot, England: Gower.

Winnicott, D. W. (1971). *Playing and reality*. London, England: Penguin.

Woodson, C. (2000). *The mis-education of the Negro*. New York, NY: African American Images.

Wynter, S. (2003, Fall). Unsettling the coloniality of being/power/truth/freedom: Towards the human, after man, its overrepresentation—an argument. *CR: The New Centennial Review, 3*(3), 257–337.

Zaal, M., Salah, T., & Fine, M. (2007). Weight of the hyphen. *Applied Developmental Science, 11*(3), 164–177.

Index

About the Author

Michelle Fine is a distinguished professor of Critical Psychology, Women's Studies, American Studies, and Urban Education at the Graduate Center, CUNY. A pioneer in the field of youth Participatory Action Research, and a founding faculty member of the Public Science Project, Fine has been involved with a series of participatory studies with youth and elders, from across different racial, ethnic, and social class backgrounds, to investigate circuits of dispossession and of critical resistance.

For her contributions to the field of Critical Psychology she has received the 2018 STAATS Award from the American Psychological Foundation for Lifetime Achievements in Science and the 2017 Award for Distinguished Contributions to Qualitative Methods from Division 5 of the American Psychological Association. She writes on the injustice of high-stakes testing and on the racial abuse and mass incarceration of people of color and queer youth, and she loves to conduct research with young people who know intimately the scars of injustice and the laughter of surviving the streets of New York.